The Best
of
Trapper John

John A. Colombo

The Best
of
Trapper John

by
John A. Colombo

Copyright 2002
ISBN 1-884687-33-4

Photographs & Illustrations
by
John A. Colombo

Published By
New Horizon Publishing Co.
P. O. Box 226
New Wilmington, Pa. 16142
(724-946-3604)

Library of Congress No. 2002101424

Second Printing 2003

FORWARD

Did you ever know anyone who seemed to know everything but turned out to be just another arrogant individual who just thought he knew everything but actually knew very little? It's disappointing. It might even make you angry. It definitely makes you reluctant to believe in those who truly do know something. Well folks, I think I know somebody who just might know everything. Ok, maybe he doesn't know everything about everything. But he sure knows a lot about an awful lot of things. You might know him too. He's Trapper John Colombo. I help him with his radio program Saturday mornings. If you have heard him on the radio, I think you might agree with me.

I haven't known Trapper John all my life. I only wish I have. Sports teams always have their "go to guy," the one guy they can count on, rely on, get the job done when there is a job that needs to be done. Trapper John is that guy.

I have a problem, though; it's hard to sit in the studio and run things with him. It's hard to focus on the mechanics of keeping a radio program on the air, like handling calls from listeners, playing commercials, keeping an eye on the time, while at the same time I'm trying to listen to what Trapper John is saying.

The answers flow from his lips like fine wine from it's bottle. Effortlessly. Confidently. Remarkably. You are often asking yourself, "How in the world does he know that?" I think that some listeners call just to offer up a good-natured challenge to Trapper John, trying to find that one question or problem he can't answer. Week in and week out, Trapper John delights his audience with his pearls of wisdom. He unselfishly offers his humble guidance to make sure there is no misstep along the way.

Trapper John is one of those unique individuals who lives up to, no, exceeds expectations. On the radio and off, he is the genuine article. Honest and straightforward. Knowledgeable and heartwarming. Like Coca Cola, he's the real thing. As people gather around the radio Saturday mornings, coffee in one hand, pencil and pad in the other, they are reminded of the good that exists in the world, and there exists out there someone who can help. This resource book will remain at arm's length of every gardener, homeowner and homebody alike. And there are some of Trapper John's favorite stories in there, too. You'll enjoy them.

My father taught me lots of thing to get me through life. Many of them he learned from his father. I'll pass them down to my son. Every family has things to pass down, so do your part-make sure you pass this down. Let the next generation appreciate what you will learn in this book. Your future generations will love you for it.   Scott Lowe

MY THANKS

This book isn't large enough to list everybody that I need to thank for helping me throughout my life. So I guess I'll just have to settle for saying thank you without listing their names, but, I'm sure you all know who you are, so, "Thank You!"

A very special thank you to my wife Audrey, who always seems to be there when I need some help, advice or comfort. It has been said that behind every good man is a better woman. I don't know if that is true in other relationships, but it's definitely true in this relationship. Thank's Sweetheart!

Last, but not least, I want to thank all of my radio listeners, without whom there wouldn't be any Trapper John, or any books either. So, Thank You, to each and every one of you.

Most of what you read in this book came from people other than myself. Yes, some of the methods and formulas are mine, but most of them came from listening to a lot of old-timers that shared their experience and knowledge with me. So, while I wrote this, I can't claim everything as my own ideas. Even though most, if not all, of those old-timers are gone now, I still feel the need to thank them for giving me their friendship and all that information to pass on.

INTRODUCTION

This book is filled with natural and/or organic methods, formulas and tips on how to do a great number of things. Most of the methods, formulas and tips were concocted using items around the house, to keep the cost down and still get good results. However, some are just going to help you do a better job, rather than cost less.

If you go over the table of contents, you will discover that the book contains tips and solutions for many different problems, and many times gives you several ways to solve those problems. You may come across some of these methods, formulas and tips elsewhere, in other books, but, I don't believe you will find any book of this type, as complete as the one in your hands.

In writing this book, I tried to include only those methods, formulas and tips that I know work at least eighty percent of the time. Naturally, there is no guarantee that using any of the formulas, methods or tips listed in this book will solve your problem.

There are far too many factors beyond my control for me to be able to offer any kind of guarantees. But, if you follow the instructions, to the letter, you should, under most circumstances, get good results. Some of the ingredients in the tips, formulas, and methods are sometimes difficult to locate. However, if you use a little ingenuity, spend a little time and make some inquires, you will find all of these items are available.

Trapper John and Audrey

Someone once said that behind every good man is a better women. I like to think that beside every good man is a better women. You've heard me refer to my wife as my "keeper" many times on my radio program, and that she is. She keeps me well dressed, well fed, happy and on the straight and narrow trail through life. Every one of you that has a good wife understands exactly what I'm saying; you that don't, well, we offer you our condolences. Be smart, go find yourself a good wife/keeper; you'll be much better off.

CAUTION

Care must be exercised whenever you are using any of the methods or tips in this book. Please use good judgement when using any of the tips, methods or advice from this book. Always, carefully follow the instruction given, doing each step, or using each item, as instructed. Never use a substitute for any ingredient given in a formula or method; it could cause problems. Always test every formula or method for staining in an inconspicuous area before using the method or formula on your rug or furniture.

Always use caution when using any products that you purchase in connection with my methods and formulas; follow the directions on the container. When using diatomaceous earth, wear a dust mask to protect your lungs from the dust particles.

The author feels that no method or formula is going to work 100% of the time. But, every method or formula in this book has worked at least 80% of the time, otherwise it wouldn't appear in the book. There is no guarantee that any of the methods or formulas in this book will solve your particular problem.

TABLE OF CONTENTS

9

ANTS

There are less than 20 species of ants that invade our homes. However, those that do invade our homes can be a real problem.

Some, like the thief ant, the pharaoh ant and the argentine ant like to get into food, especially sweet stuff. These are all small ants, ranging in size up to ⅛ inch long. You can combat these ants with a product called "TERRO."

Follow the instructions on the container for the best results. And, don't keep killing ants when you are using this product! The ants carry the TERRO back to the nest to feed to the larvae. This normally eliminates the entire colony, sometimes within several weeks, while at other times it may take several months. The time necessary to completely eliminate a colony depends on the size of the colony, so be patient!

Other ants, such as the carpenter ant, don't bother food, but will burrow in the wood in your home. They don't eat the wood, they just chew holes in it to make their home. Since they don't eat the wood, you will always find sawdust where they are working.

By the way, termites do eat the wood, so there isn't any sawdust when they invade your home. If you think your problem is termites, you better contact a professional. Termites can do an extensive amount of damage in a very short time. While you are thinking things over, they could eat your house.

You can get rid of most of the larger types of ants by using diatomaceous earth, or rotenone dust, around where you see them. In new construction, it's a good idea to put DE (diatomaceous earth) in between all the studs in the outside walls of the house before installing the plaster board. You should drop some down into the cement block walls of the basement before the plate is installed. This stuff keeps killing bugs forever. DE is over a million years old and still kills insects.

In older homes, it's a good idea to put some DE on the plate in the basement; that's the board at the top of the concrete block wall in the basement that I just spoke of above. You should also put some in the walls where the pipes are - under the sinks in the kitchen or bathroom. Just pull the metal ring away from the wall and put it in with a plastic mustard bottle.

Get an empty mustard squeeze bottle and pry the cone top off, then cut the plug off that seals the cone shut when you turn it down on the cap. Now wash, dry and fill the bottle with diatomaceous earth. Hold it with the nozzle down for a second, then aim it and squeeze sharply. Works great as a dispenser!

Back to the job at hand. Under the kitchen cabinets, in the kick plate, you should drill some ¾ inch holes, apply the diatomaceous earth and then insert some fascia plugs. Fascia plugs can be purchased from a lumber company in various colors to match your kick plate.

Ants that you find coming up in the cracks between your sidewalk and driveway slabs, can be controlled with pure chlorine bleach, vinegar or boiling water. Just pour it right in the cracks. And be generous! It's cheap!

If your problem is with ants building mounds in your yard, you can eliminate them with Tide laundry detergent - powder or liquid. The basic formula is two cups of Tide in one gallon of boiling water. Stir until the detergent is suspended in the water and you have a milky liquid. Depending on the size of the mound, you may need to mix up to five gallons to do the job.

While you are waiting for the mixture to cool, take a shovel and scoop up the mound down to the level of the surrounding soil. Throw each shovel of soil with the wind, as far as you can. This way the ants you scoop up cannot get back to the colony to re-establish it. Ants travel by laying a trail of pheromone (a scent they emit that is specific to their colony only), to find their way back to the colony. When you throw them, they don't have a trail to follow back to the colony.

When the liquid is cool enough to handle, pour it in a circular movement from the outside diameter of the mound base to the inside, saturating the soil thoroughly. You can wet the area down, after you pour the mixture on, if necessary, with an equal amount of water.
Never use more water than mixture, you will dilute the mixture too much and it will not work.

Next, cover the area of the mound with a plastic lawn or garbage bag and hold it down with some stones or pieces of wood. Tomorrow, you can pick up the plastic bag - the colony is dead. If you don't feel like going to all of this trouble and would rather spend some money to do it the easy way, buy a bottle of Hot Pepper Wax Brand Insect Repellent. Saturate the ant hill, after you level it as per the instructions above, with a 32 to 1 mixture. The next day hose the area down well. You may need to repeat the process again, two days later, to completely eliminate the colony.

You can make a good ant bait as follows:

1 cup warm water
½ cup sugar
2 teaspoons boric acid
some cotton

Mix the boric acid and sugar, then dissolve them in warm water. Soak some cotton in the mixture and place it loosely in a screw-top container. (Small baby food jars work great.) Put the lid on tightly and punch several ¼ inch entrance holes in the lid so the ants can reach the bait. The ants will take the bait home for food, thus killing the colony over several weeks/months time, depending on the size of the colony.

A very good spray for ants around the outside of the house is insecticidal soap. You can purchase this at any good Lawn & Garden store, or Nursery. Just follow the instructions on the container, as to the mixture to spray.

Remember, nature never lets you win the war, only some of the battles. When you realize that you have gotten rid of all of the ants, be prepared, new ants will move in eventually, maybe not this summer, but soon. Keeps life interesting, doesn't it?

By the way, ants have three separate and distinct sections to their body; the head, the thorax and the abdomen. The thorax and abdomen are attached by a thin hair like waist.

Termites on the other hand, have three sections that are not so separate. Their head, thorax and abdomen are all connected. There isn't any hair like waist or neck. Termites and ants are not the same. Ants are from the order Hymenoptera while termites are from the order Isoptera.

Most ants will either bite or sting you if you disturb them. Others just emit a foul smelling secretion when annoyed. They vary quite a lot in their habits, some are carnivorous, some are scavengers, while others eat plants.

COCKROACHES

This household pest is hard to get rid of, unless you are willing to go to extreme measures. Cockroaches feed on just about anything. When it's dark and quiet they forage for food, especially while you are sleeping. During the day, they hide in cracks, under baseboards, behind cabinets; anywhere they can get into the darkness. They normally have an unpleasant odor.

Adult cockroaches live approximately 200 days; the egg stage is 23 days, the nymph stage is anywhere from 30 to 100 days. The female produces around four egg cases containing 30 to 50 eggs each.

The first thing you must do is to clean the entire house thoroughly with a good disinfectant soap and water. Chlorine bleach in your water also helps to disinfect the house and kill any eggs or larvae it contacts.

Next, you should vacuum every crack to pick up any hiding roaches. But, first put a three inch piece of flea collar in the sweeper bag; this kills the roaches and nymphs you vacuum up.

Once this is done, you must fill every crack, nook or cranny with a good silicone caulk, to eliminate places for the roaches to hide and lay eggs. If you use a clear caulk, it's not noticeable, unless you are looking for it.

Spread diatomaceous earth, or agricultural boric acid, under free standing cabinets, behind, in and under the kitchen cabinets, and under your appliances.

Drill holes ¾ inch in diameter in the kick plate of the kitchen cabinets and squirt some of the powder in there. Then use fascia board plugs to seal the holes, while allowing for ventilation. Put some in the walls by removing the outlet and switch plates, and squirting the powder into the wall with an old mustard squeeze bottle.

The squeeze bottle is made by removing the funnel top on the mustard bottle and cutting off the plug that seals the bottle when the nozzle is screwed down, then putting the nozzle top back on and screwing it down tight. You can then screw the top off and fill the bottle with the powder. To apply, simply squeeze the bottle quickly.

Some good cockroach killing baits can be made as follows:

Formula #1
1 tablespoon powdered sugar
1 tablespoon alum
1 tablespoon white flour
1 tablespoon boric acid
the juice of one small onion

Mix all of the ingredients together with just enough cooking oil to make a stiff dough. Roll into balls about half the size of a BB and put them where the roaches can get to them.

Formula #2
1 oz. Trisodium Phosphate
1 oz. Salicylic Acid
6 oz. Borax
4 oz. Sugar
8 oz. White Flour

Mix thoroughly and dust where you think the roaches will get into the powder. Keep this dry. If it gets wet, or cakes, throw it away and make a new batch.

A good cockroach trap can be made using a small jar, a piece of banana and some Vaseline. Place the banana in the center, bottom of the jar and then, using the Vaseline, coat the inside of the jar mouth and down inside the jar as far as you can. Place the jar near a wall where the roaches will try to get the banana.

Another good trap is made with a piece of duct tape and a banana. Tear off a piece of tape six or eight inches long and smear some banana down the center of the sticky side and place next to the wall. The roaches will stick to the tape and you can drop them in boiling water to kill them.

Always make sure there isn't any garbage left in the house. After every meal take the scraps, etc., outside to the garbage can and immediately wash and dry all of the pans, dishes and utensils used.

If everything is kept clean, all the cracks are filled and all garbage is removed, there won't be anything for the roaches to eat, and no place to hide or lay eggs.

Even after you think you have gotten rid of all of the roaches, set out one of the above traps to make sure. Sometimes you can have a few roaches and not see any of them, until the few bred and turn into many.

OSAGE ORANGES

This is the fruit of the Osage Orange tree - a large convoluted green ball ranging from the size of a tennis ball up to a large grapefruit. This fruit has the ability to repel insects, if you get it after the frost has knocked it from the tree. When picked before a killing frost, the fruit will rot and draw fruit flies.

When picked up from the ground after a killing frost has knocked them from the tree, they will deteriorate - giving off an essence that will repel insects from your home.

You will know when the fruit is not doing the job, because it will grow a cottony fungus all over the out side of the fruit. The fungus is either white or gray, and looks and feels like cotton. If this fungus starts to grow over more than a very small part of the fruit, get rid of it, or you will have fruit flies shortly.

Never throw the fruit away just because it looks like it is rotten. This is the process that emits the essence that repels the insects. The fruit will get brown, yellow, black and white spots all over it as it deteriorates, but will not grow the cotton fungus, because it's working properly.

For over a hundred years now, people have been using this fruit to get rid of flies, spiders, roaches, crickets and all kinds of other insects that have invaded their homes. Try some, you will be glad you did.

If you get small ones, you will need one in each corner of a room 9' X 12'. But, with large ones you will only need two in the same size room. You will have to figure out how many you need for the entire house.

Some folks put them in the basement and then wonder why the house is infested with spiders and other bugs. Because, the essence drove them upstairs! If you use this method, either place the fruit upstairs where you live or do as we do, put some in every room, and the basement.

When placing this fruit around your home, always put the fruit in, or on, something so as not to stain the carpets or flooring. We use those small aluminum pie plates. They work great - just the right size for either the small or large fruits.

Also, always place the fruits on the floor, so the essence can rise up and fill the entire area.

Never buy Osage Oranges from a flea market person, unless you know they are honest.

Many flea market vendors just pick the oranges from the tree and really don't care if they work or not; they are only interested in getting your money. One time I watched 2 fellows fill a pickup truck with oranges they picked from a tree. Two days later, I saw them selling the fruit at a flea market.

One last thought on Osage Oranges. If you locate a tree, don't tell anybody where it is or you will find that you won't get any of the fruit; everyone else will have taken all of the fruit for themselves, their family and friends. Trust me, keep the location a secret! Then you can give some of your fruit to whomever you wish and still have enough for yourself.

ALUMINUM CLEANER

You can shine aluminum with the following mixture:

¾ cup caulk (calcium carbonate)
½ cup cheap talcum powder
½ cup alum

Mix thoroughly, then dip a damp cloth into the mix and rub the item vigorously. Rinse with clean water and dry with a soft cloth.

If the aluminum is really crusty, you will have to clean it before you can polish it. You can purchase a good cleaner in most Auto Parts Stores. Ask for a good aluminum wheel cleaner.

To remove dark discolorations from aluminum utensils, try putting a tablespoon of Calgon in the utensil and fill it with water. Bring the water to a boil and then simmer it for three minutes, or so, and the spots will be gone.

Following is a very good aluminum cleaner and polish: Dissolve a ½ ounce of trisodium phosphate in 24 ounces of water. Stir in 2 fluid ounces of water glass (Sodium Silicate) and sift in 4 ounces of fine Tripoli powder (rottenstone). Because Tripoli doesn't dissolve, you must agitate the liquid as you bottle it. Shake well before using and apply with a soft cloth, rubbing in only one direction. Polish with a clean soft cloth.

DRAIN CLEANER

Drains becoming sluggish is usually an indication that there is a build up of hardened grease, hair and lint in the drain. To correct this problem, pour one half cup of baking soda down the sink drain and follow with one half cup of vinegar.

Let it work for fifteen minutes or so, then flush the drain with boiling water. It's noisy, but won't hurt your pipes, so don't get excited!

The basic ingredient in most drain cleaners is sodium hydroxide(lye). This is sometimes mixed with a substance that will cause it to have a turbulent cleaning action.

A good way to prevent drain clogging is to give your drains a weekly treatment of either lye, washing soda, or the formula above. Should you use the lye, put a tablespoon (be sure to wash the spoon) in the drain sieve and flush it down with a cup of very hot water. Allow it to work for 5, or so, minutes then flush well with warm water.

If you decide to use the washing soda, put 3 tablespoons in the drain basket and slowly run very hot water into the basket until the soda is gone.

To open a clogged drain, remove as much of the water in the sink and drain as is possible. Then slowly dissolve one small can (13 oz.)of lye in 2 quarts of cold water, in either a glass or stainless container. Stir with a plastic or wooden spoon. The lye will heat up the solution. Pour it down the drain slowly and carefully. Wait 10 minutes and flush the drain well, with water.

CAUTION: Lye is caustic and poison. If you spill it on your skin or surrounding objects, wash immediately with plenty of cold water.

KEEPING GARLIC

Our neighbor, Marge Valentine, stores her garlic by grinding it and freezing it in ½ oz containers. She then opens them as needed. We tried it and it works great.

LEMONS

You will get more juice from your citrus fruit if you microwave them for 20 to 30 seconds before you squeeze them.
Don't forget to pierce the skin first. Always roll the lemon, with your hand, on the counter before squeezing.

To add flavor and keep your chicken moist during roasting, slip some lemon slices under the breast skin before roasting.

To enhance the flavor of a dull pudding, grate a little zest from a lemon over the pudding and stir in before cooking. By the way, zest is finely grated lemon peel.

Don't throw away your lemon after squeezing the juice out, use it dipped in salt to clean and shine your copper bottomed pots. You'll be delighted with the results.

It you like to drink tea, you will love tea seasoned with zesty sugar. Mix 1 or 2 tablespoons of yellow lemon zest in a cup of granulated sugar and allow it to set for a week or so before using it. By the way, this tastes good on custards or in salads also.

If your blond hair is looking kind of dull, use a lemon juice rinse to brighten it. Squeeze the juice of one lemon into a cup of water, work this into your hair and allow it to work for several minutes, then rinse your hair with warm water. You'll look great!

WOOD BURNING

If you burn wood in a fireplace or stove, you can help to keep the chimney clean by setting a box of kitchen salt on the hot coals as the fire burns down. Do this once or twice every month and your chimney will need cleaning only in the spring or fall of each year.

Some folks like to store some wood in the basement so they always have dry wood to use. This wood is replaced as they use it. The wood is normally brought into the basement on Saturday and used the following week. As the wood warms up, the insects laying dormant under the bark start moving out into the basement and become a problem.

You can stop them in their tracks by putting down a layer of diatomaceous earth before you start piling up your logs. Each layer of logs should be dusted with diatomaceous earth to catch the insects as they emerge from under the bark.

The nice thing about using diatomaceous earth is that it won't harm you or your pets if they get into it - as long as they or you are not breathing the dust.
(All dust is harmful to your lungs - even flour!!)

FLEAS

Black walnut leaves, cedar chips, pine needles, salt and chamomile leaves, all repel fleas. If you have a dog or cat, you can place some of any of these in the animal's bed and keep it free of fleas.

Put a few drops of pine needle oil, cedar oil or lavender oil in your animal's rinse water and you can keep it flea free, provided you wash the animal on a regular schedule and use the oil.

Rubbing alcohol, when sprayed on your dog or cat as you thumb the hair up so it reaches the skin, will kill any fleas on the animal, but burns like the devil if it gets into a cut or scrape - so be careful.

Flea eggs hatch approximately every seven days or so, and the larvae will feed on any organic matter available.

In about thirty days, they pupate in silken cocoons and may remain dormant for months, waiting until stimulated by vibrations indicating that a host may be present.

Adults, unlike the larvae, suck the blood of their host. After feeding, the adults breed and the females lay up to 500 eggs before they die. If well fed, fleas have a life span of up to 18 months.

Put a two inch piece of flea collar in your sweeper bag and every flea, or any insect, you vacuum up will die before it can escape from the bag.

If you have a pet, you should make a flea trap. The following flea trap has worked well for me for over forty years. Try making one yourself; it's a cheap way to solve a problem before it gets out of hand.

Instructions: Take a Clorox gallon jug, view it as square and cut a four inch diameter hole in each side (you will have four holes).

Make sure the bottom of the holes are approximately one and a half inches up from the bottom of the jug. Stick a welcome light, light first, down the neck of the jug. To use the trap, put an inch of water in the bottom and five or six drops of dishwashing soap. Stir the water to mix in the soap, plug in the light and go to bed. In the morning you will see dots of pepper in the water - fleas that drown. Just dump out the water and set the trap aside for next time

ONIONS

You won't cry as much when peeling onions if you place them in the freezer for fifteen minutes, or the refrigerator thirty minutes, before you begin peeling them. If you forget, just sprinkle a little vinegar on the cutting board - it helps some.

Want to make your onions easy to peel? Just drop them in boiling water for ten seconds, then in cold water and peel.

If you like onion powder, why not make your own. Slice the onions and place in either a dehydrator or your oven (set at the lowest heat) and dry throughly. When dry, use a blender or food processor to make powder. Keep homemade onion powder in the refrigerator.

GLASS CLEANER

You can make several good glass cleaners as follows:

Formula #1
½ cup ammonia
½ cup vinegar
½ gallon water

Mix and put some in a spray bottle to use. Store the rest, to refill the bottle as needed.
Shake well before spraying the window, then wipe with newspaper or paper towel.

Formula #2
½ cup of corn starch
½ gallon of warm water

Mix these thoroughly and shake well before using. One of my listeners uses this and said it works better that anything he has ever tried.

To keep your windows from being streaked when you clean them, put a few drops of "Jet Dry" in your cleaning solution. Try that one - you' ll like it.
Also, your windows will clean better if you wipe them dry with newspaper or paper toweling rather than a rag.

MOSQUITOES

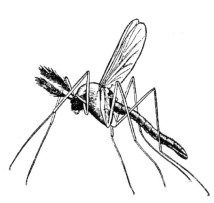

If you are having problems with mosquitoes in and around your yard and you don't live next to a swamp, try spraying the grass and shrubs in your yard with one of the insect soap sprays.
This is easily accomplished by using a hose end sprayer with the ability to adjust the mixture, such as the one put out by Hot Pepper Wax. This will get rid of the mosquitoes, fleas, and a lot of the other insect pests in the yard.

I've found that by spraying myself with some SUPERSHIELD GREEN, a product produced   by the company ABSORBINE, the mosquitoes just leave me alone.

By the way, SUPERSHIELD GREEN is completely natural. Try it, you will be glad you did.

If you can't get some SuperShield Green, just rub yourself with lavender oil.

A drop of ammonia on a mosquito bite stops the itch.

The foam type sheets ladies put in the dryer, called Bounce, also repel insects.   Some of these strategically placed on you, like on your shirt collar, sleeve cuffs and your hat, should be very effective against mosquitoes.

If you have some stagnant water around your home, you can kill mosquito larvae, and not harm the environment, by spreading cooking oil on the water.

SLIPPERY WALKS

Salt and Sodium are corrosive and kill your grass. Urea fertilizer melts ice and feeds your grass, and isn't corrosive. Not too expensive either.

SLUGS & SNAILS

 If something is eating your plants and you never see anything on the plants, you can always tell if the problem is slugs because they leave a slimy mucus trail on the soil, and sometimes on the plant leaves.

If insects are doing the damage, you will not see this slime trail. The slime looks shiny with several reddish colors when it dries. It's easier to see the slime trail if you try to look at an angle, by getting down close to the soil or leaf you're checking.

To solve your problem, just spread some coarse sand, diatomaceous earth, hydrated lime, wood ashes or pine bark mulch around the base of the plant, and the slugs won't cross it.

Be sure not to spread the lime around plants that like an acid soil. For acid-loving plants, try spreading some cottonseed meal.

You might just go out to the garden at night and pick the slugs from your plants and drop them into a jar of kerosene, or soapy water, or sprinkle them with salt. While working in the garden, always carry a salt shaker with you and sprinkle some salt on the slugs when you find them. It kills them quickly!

Spraying your plants with Hot Pepper Wax Brand Insect Repellent, at a ratio of 16 to 1, will stop the slugs also.

A well manicured garden has far less problems with snails and slugs. Pick up all of the litter and dead plant material. Don't let boards, or that type of thing, lay around for slugs and snails to hide under.

Eating grapefruit for breakfast? Save the rinds and put them, cut side down, in the garden, being sure to prop one side up with a small pebble. Tomorrow morning pick up the rind and it will be full of slugs. You can kill them and use the rind again, if you want to, or just drop the rind into some kerosene.

Orange rind works almost as good. Try it!

WASPS

Wasps normally will not bother you unless they are disturbed. They are not as aggressive as yellow jackets. These fellows are predators. They eat lots of insects around your home, so if you can get along without killing them, it's best to do so.

However, if you really need to get rid of them, try some of the following methods.

You can stop wasps from building hives in the eves of your home by tacking up some mothballs.

Just cut some six inch squares from old nylon stockings and wrap four or five mothballs in the nylon and staple, or tack them on the wall and the soffit. They should be spaced about four or five feet apart.

One fellow said he used two sided tape to put one mothball every 10 or 12 inches and that worked great for him. When one dissolved, he just stuck up another one.

If they are getting into your attic, spread cedar shavings along the inside where the roof rafters touch the walls. You need a strip about eighteen inches wide, from the roof line out toward the center of the house, and get some into the soffit, if possible.

If they are building hives in a location you can't get to, try soaking a rag in kerosene and put it as close to the hive as you can, preferable under it, with a long pole. They can't breath because of the fumes from the kerosene, so they should move someplace else.

After they leave, you can destroy the hive to keep them from returning to it. (See hornets and yellow jackets for more tips.)

Remember, the more wasps you kill during August and September, the less wasps you will have to contend with next year. The last hatch of the season produces the wasps that winter over and start the new hives next spring

CUT FLOWERS

Your cut flowers will last longer if you drop a plain aspirin into the vase of water with them.

HORNETS

Hornets are the most defensive of all the stinging bees. If you stand back away from their hive and watch it, you will notice that they have sentries posted around the opening. When something comes near the hive, they will fly toward it, trying to get it to leave.

If this doesn't work, they attack and sting the invader. Usually, this is sufficient to make the invader leave. However, if it stays near, the colony will attack in force!

If you have the nerve, and can reach the hive, you can destroy their colony with Automobile Starting Fluid. Wait until it is dark, then take your starting fluid and hold it under the opening in the hive. Press the button- spraying into the opening. Keep spraying until the can is empty - then walk away immediately.

In the morning you can watch the hive from a distance, for a few minutes, and when you are satisfied they are all dead, tear down the hive.

If the hive is smaller than a basketball, and is low enough, you can soak a rag in kerosene and hang it right above the hive so it drips down on it. Do this after dark, and this will also make them leave, provided enough kerosene drips onto the hive. This works because it effects their breathing.
(See wasps and yellow jackets also.)

Hornets are predators, so don't kill them unless you have no other choice - they eat lots of insects.

Always destroy, in the winter, any hives you find around your home so they can't re-establish them come spring. In the spring if the queen finds a hive, she can spend more time laying eggs and taking care of the larvae that emerge first. This allows her to build a much larger colony than she could if she was forced to build her own hive.

If they are building hives under the soffit on your house, there is an easy way to stop them. In the spring when they start coming around, cut some 6" squares of nylon from old stockings. Place 3 or 4 mothballs on the nylon, gather the edges and staple the make-shift bags under the soffit against the wall. Space these at 3 or 4 foot intervals from one side to the other. If you do this every year, you won't have any of these guys building hives around your place ever again.

YELLOW JACKETS

Normally these fellows live in hives attached to the underside of the roof rafters, inside the soffit and fascia on your house or garage, or under your deck. However, yellow jackets sometimes live in the ground or hanging hives, similar to those made by hornets.

When they are living underground, you can eliminate them by soaking the ground with boiling water. Or, you can fill a sixteen ounce soda bottle with kerosene, force the neck of the bottle into the entrance hole so it stays there, and go to bed.

Wait several days before you pick up your bottle, that way you can be sure the hive is dead. That is, if you did the job right. If not, do it again.

Notice, I said go to bed, because you shouldn't do any of these methods while it's daylight. Wait until after dark!

Yellow Jackets drink nectar and feed their larvae pre-chewed insects. They can be real pests at a picnic, trying to carry off small bits of food. If you interfere and try to chase them away, they sting you. Guess they think it's their picnic.

You can make a good yellow jacket trap from a two litter soda bottle and a 12" piece of ¾" PVC pipe.

Cut the ends of the pipe at a 45° angle, then with the angles up, in the center of the pipe, on the under side, cut or drill a ⅜" hole. Next, cut holes in the sides of the bottle for the pipe to fit through - about half way up from the bottom of the bottle. Fit the pipe in the bottle so the ⅜ hole is centered and the angles face up. Put some apple juice in the bottle, cap it, and place it away from where the picnic will be held. Put a few drops of juice on the lid to attract them to the trap.

Now comes the time for you to play god. You can either remove the lid and allow them to live, or you can drop the trap in a bucket of water and kill them.....your decision.

Be sure to check out the method for keeping hornets from building hives under the soffit - it works for these fellows too.

INSECTICIDE

You can make your own insecticide as follows:
- 1 cup of Ivory laundry soap
- 1 gallon of boiling water
- 1 pint of kerosene

To the boiling water, add the Ivory soap - stirring constantly. When the soap is suspended in the water, remove from the stove and place on the floor.

Now, slowly pour in the kerosene while stirring the solution until all the kerosene is absorbed by the liquid. NEVER POUR KEROSENE IN THE SOLUTION WHILE IT IS ON THE STOVE!! Allow this to cool before using. If you have done everything right, you will have a milky solution. To use, add one cup to a gallon of water and spray your plants, or whatever you want to protect. Remember, some plants are tender and can't take all sprays.

For another good insecticide, peal and soak one crushed garlic bulb, not just a clove, in a pint of rubbing alcohol for five days. Remove the garlic and add one half cup of cooking oil, a tablespoon of red pepper, one tablespoon of dishwashing soap and one cup of water. Let this mixture set for approximately twelve hours before you use it. Do not dilute it, and shake well before using.

BRASS POLISH

Need some brass polish? Just put a tablespoon of salt in half a cup of vinegar and add enough flour to make a paste. Dip a damp cloth into the paste and rub the brass until bright. Rinse with cold water.

This works for copper also.

When you want to make clean brass sparkle, dip a damp cloth in ketchup and rub throughly, then rinse in warm water.

To remove spots, use an old toothbrush and some toothpaste before applying polish.

BROKEN KEY

If you break your key off in a lock, don't worry, just slip an old jigsaw blade in beside the key; turn the blade so the teeth grab the key and pull it out. You may need to use a pair of pliers to twist and pull the jigsaw blade out If your jigsaw uses the type of blade with the cross pin in each end, just break one end off where the teeth start.

MOUSE TRAP

I'll bet you didn't know that your wire screened minnow trap makes an excellent mouse trap. Just hang the bait inside and prop it with something to keep it from rolling around.

The mice go in through the funnel and can't get back out. When ready, just drop the trap in a bucket of water to do away with the mice. If you are into trapping fox or coyotes, place your trap outside to catch field mice for bait to use while trapping.

Some years back, I came up with a bucket trap for catching mice. You need a 5 gallon bucket with approximately 4" of water in it, a wire coat hanger, a tomato soup can and a board. Cut or drill some holes in your can of soup to drain the contents, making sure not to ruin the center of the top and bottom. When it's empty and clean, drill an ⅛" hole in the center of the top and bottom.

Cut the coat hanger and slip it through the holes you just made in the can. Now bend it into a U shape that just fits inside the bucket.

Next, bend the ends of the wire over to hold the can just below the rim of the bucket. Take your board and prop it up against the bucket, making a ramp for the mice to walk up. The ramp must allow the mouse to see the can from the side. Rap a piece of raw bacon around the can and fasten it with some twine.

Now the mice will walk up the ramp, see and smell the bacon, and try to jump on the can to eat it. Their weight, as they land, will cause the can to spin around, dropping them into the water to drown.

If you are using this trap at a camp, or some place that you can only empty the bucket once a week, float about an inch of cooking oil on the water to keep the odor down. The oil will coat that part of the mice sticking out of the water and seal in most of the odor.

CAST IRON UTENSILS

When your cast iron skillets, or pots, need to be re-seasoned and you want to season them like they did in the old days, just rub a thin coating of some lard on them and set them in the center of a bonfire.

When the fire goes out and cools down, retrieve your cast iron utensil and it's ready to use, after wiping with a damp cloth.

If you can't wait for a bonfire, rub a thin coating of lard on your utensil, put it in the oven, set on 500°, and bake the cast iron utensil for several hours. Turn off the oven and let it cool to room temperature before removing the cast iron utensil.

If your range has a high temperature cleaning cycle, your can put the cast iron utensil in the oven and season it while you are cleaning the oven. Be sure to set the cast iron utensil on an iron trivet in the oven to do the seasoning.

To clean the cast iron utensil before seasoning it, if needed, just boil some vinegar and salt in it, until it comes clean. This usually only needs to be done on new utensils that have some kind of rust preventative on them

If necessary, use a steel wool pad to remove any gunk you can't get off with just a rag, on older utensils that you are re-seasoning. If that doesn't do the job, as a last resort, you can use a 4" angle grinder with a wire brush to really clean off the crud on your cast iron utensils.

Once you have finished seasoning your iron utensil, never use metal spoons, etc., as they will cut the finish and this is what is causing the food you cook to stick to the bottom. Wooden or plastic spoons, etc., will not cut the finish.

I've heard of people using oil to season their utensils. Since I personally only use lard, I can't comment on this method. If you try it and it works for you, let me know.

FROZEN LOCK

Heat the key with a match or lighter and insert it into the lock. May take several tries, but does work.

FLIES

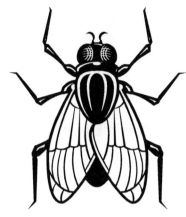

Flies bothering you? You better purchase a bottle of "A B S O R B I N E ' S S U P E R S H I E L D GREEN".
This stuff was formulated to keep flies from driving horses crazy, however, it works great on you and me too.

In tests I ran, SUPERSHIELD worked really well as an insect repellant. I can put some on and fish all evening without getting bit.

And the best part of all, it's natural, all organic, no harsh chemicals! This stuff is really great for black flies.

If the flies are bothering you around the kitchen, just add a couple of drops of lavender oil to a small glass of boiling water and place it on the table. (I've been told that placing several drops of lavender oil on a lit light bulb will fill the area with the scent, and repel insects. While I haven't tried this, it sounds like it should work.) Flies leave, and the house smells great!

Cluster flies in the attic can be controlled by using some Malrin Fly Bait. You can't buy dispensers any more, so I make my own from two liter soda bottles. Look at the bottle as though it were square. Now, cut a 2 inch diameter hole in each of the four sides. The top edge of the holes should be in line with the top of the label. Next, drill a small hole in the lid, install a wire, or string, through the lid, to hang your bait station. Fill the bottle up to the holes with fly bait, put the lid on and hang it up in the attic, or wherever you think the flies will find it.

Be sure to replenish the bait as they eat it - even in the winter. On warm days during the winter, the flies start moving around and will come to the bait because they need to eat, and, of course, the bait kills them.

In the spring when they gather on the sunny outside of the house, use your Hot Pepper Wax hose end sprayer, filled with Tide laundry detergent, powder or liquid, and spray the outside walls of the house to kill them.

Keeping a bait station somewhere outside the house, near where the flies gather, is a good idea, in the spring and summer. Cover the openings with ½" hardware cloth to keep the birds and animals from eating the bait and dying. You can keep the hardware cloth in place with Duct tape. You might want to add a tin pie pan as a roof over the bait station, to keep the rain from ruining your bait. The way I do this is to drill a hole just large enough for the hanging wire from the lid to slip through, in the center of the pie plate. Slip the wire through the hole and put some good glue on the lid, before you push them together. Then add a small amount of glue where the wire comes out of the pie plate. Now the lid is fastened down tight enough to stay in place, and no rain can go down the wire and into the bait.

I used to keep several of these around the yard all spring and summer when we first moved into the farm. We had so many cluster flies that you would think we were breeding them. Even with all of the effort and work we applied to this job, it still took almost 4 years to eliminate the problem. I guess what I'm saying is, keep at it, eventually you will win, even though it doesn't look that way.

YARD INSECTS

Many times you have problems with different types of insects invading your yard; such as fleas, gnats, mosquitoes, beetles, etc. A very good way to keep the numbers of these invaders down is to hose down the yard with an insecticidal soap spray.

Just fill the bottle on your Hot Pepper Wax hose end sprayer with one of the concentrated insecticidal soaps. Set the dial for a mixture of thirty two to one, put the nozzle on fan and spray to your hearts content.

If you do this several times during the summer, you'll have a lot less insects to deal with around the yard. And while you are spraying the lawn, don't forget to do the bushes and trees on the property, if you haven't already done these before.

You don't need to keep your kids, or pets, away from the lawn for several days either. Just make them wait until the grass is dry so you don't have to wash their grubby clothes, and they don't drink any of the solution.

CENTIPEDES & MILLIPEDES

Most folks call these critters "Thousand Leggers" and you usually find them around damp places, because that is where they like to hide when not hunting.

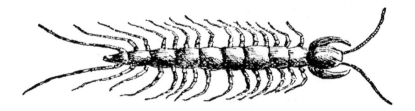

That's one good reason why you find them in the bathroom, kitchen and laundry.

The one most people see around the house is the common house centipede, or Scutigera Coleoptrata. Actually, he's one of the good guys! He's a predator. He hunts for, kills, and eats insects and spiders. They have 15 pairs of legs, one for each segment of their body, which makes me wonder why people call them thousand leggers??

Millipedes have two pair of legs per segment, are dark brown, move very slowly and don't eat insects.
The centipede has one pair of legs per segment, is predacious and eats plenty of pests around the house, like flies, fleas and other insects.

They don't get into food, unless there are insect pests in the food already. Then they are just there to get a meal.

And, they don't normally bite people, so I can't think of any good reason to go around killing them, especially since they are working for me, killing other pests I'd rather not have in my house. Ok, so you got bit! I didn't say that they never bite anyone, I said they don't normally bite.

Millipedes don't normally come into the house unless they are driven in because the soil gets saturated and they must leave, or drown. Then, because they can't survive unless it is damp, and basements are usually dry, they die anyway, in a very short time.

PESTICIDES

Unfortunately, we live in a time when everybody wants results yesterday. Some feel, to hell with waiting for results and who cáres about the damage we might cause the environment by our impatience! In many areas of our country you can't drink water from a well because the aquifer is polluted because of all the chemicals we use.

But I care, and hopefully you care, enough to start using natural pesticides instead of the harmful chemicals we see in all the stores. Don't misunderstand me, I'm not saying we can do without chemicals. What I'm saying is that we tend to use way more than is necessary, and much stronger chemical solutions than is needed for the job at hand-if enough is good, more is better...right?...WRONG!

There are plenty of good natural pesticides available, but they take a little longer to do the job. There are both organic and inorganic pesticides on the market.

Some of the inorganic pesticides I recommend are boric acid, copper, sulfur, silica and diatomaceous earth. Sulfur comes in different types of powder, some are wettable, and can be mixed with water and sprayed, while others must be dusted. Copper comes in both a powder and a liquid. All the others are powders, however occasionally some can be found in wettable powders.

Pesticide soaps have been around for a century, or so, and are usually sodium or potassium salts combined with oil and water. Oil based pesticides have been in use for many years, mostly as dormant oil sprays. However, with the new research and technologies we now have available, there are oil sprays that you can use all year round.

Then we have the botanical insecticides, such as pyrethrum, nicotine, rotenone, sabadilla and more. Of course, there are studies and experiments going on around the county all the time and I wouldn't be surprised to hear of more new organic insecticides being found in the near future, especially if more people start buying only organic and natural products and refuse to use harmful chemicals.

I believe we started using chemicals because they were cheap to produce, and the big companies pushed their use because of the profits involved. Now we know they are not as cheap as we thought, and cause lots of problems to our health and the environment.

You can make some pretty good insecticides just using the products you have at home.

Try this one next time you need something to do away with a few insects.

> 1 cup of any dishwashing soap.
> 1 cup of any cooking oil.
> 1 tablespoon of garlic oil.
> 1 cup rubbing alcohol.

Dilute one cup of this mixture in a half gallon of water and spray. Remember, most organic sprays don't have a very long residual effect, so spray on a regular schedule.

There are many plants that will repel insects, so check out some of the books on companion planting at the local library to see which will work for you.

Remember, using chemicals is not always a bad thing. Sometimes there isn't any other recourse to solve a problem. But, if you must use a harsh chemical to solve your problem, be sure you use only what is necessary and don't subscribe to the old adage that, "more is better!" More is not better. That philosophy, I believe, is what got us into trouble to begin with. So be judicious in your use of any pesticides.

FUNGUS

Fungus can be a problem in many ways, such as around the house or in the garden. And, depending where your problem is, you will need to follow directions and use different solutions.

When you are having problems with some fungus attacking your plants, try this one: Soak a bulb of garlic in a quart of rubbing alcohol for twenty four hours. Remove the garlic and spray the plant with a mixture of one cup of the alcohol solution, diluted in one quart of water.

Store the balance of the alcohol for later use, but be sure the bottle is sealed and marked as to its contents, because you don't want to get this on your skin!

For a mild case of fungus on a plant, a tablespoon or two of baking soda dissolved in a pint of warm water will often solve the problem. You can also spray, or dust, with liquid, or powder, sulfur or copper. For fungus growing on your lawn, they make a product that works fairly well.

If your problem is the moss growing on your roof, that isn't a fungus, so you need to treat it differently. There are a number of products on the market that will kill the moss growing on your roof.

Personally I like to use chlorine bleach. Usually, I find two cups of chlorine bleach in a gallon of water will kill the moss. However, if the moss has been allowed to get very thick, it gets real stubborn and then I use the chlorine bleach straight from the bottle. And if it's really thick(stubborn), you may have to apply the chlorine bleach two or three times over the next several days.

PANTRY PESTS

Seems like more and more people are having trouble with insects in their grain or seed products. Insects like the flour moth, the Indian  meal moth or any one of the assortment of beetles and weevils that attack food products in grain mills, bakeries, warehouses and grocery stores can come home with you when you make a purchase from one of these places.

Yes, I said grocery stores; that's where some of these insects get into your food products. Normally, they arrive at the grocery store in some seed or grain product that was shipped from an infested warehouse somewhere. Unfortunately, the grocer didn't know there was a problem ....until you tell him!

So, if you bring this problem home, try to immediately 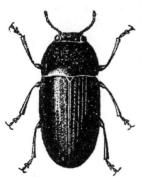 identify where you purchased the product. Then go and tell the store owner so that he can try to stop the problem from spreading. You might want to take the package with you to get a refund.

These insects aren't sitting around in your kitchen just waiting for you to bring something home for them to eat. They came in the product, from the store.

Unfortunately, you don't always find them soon enough to nip the problem in the bud. Once they get a foothold in your kitchen, you will be in for a really tough time trying to eliminate them.

There are over two hundred different species of insects that live in, and eat, stored food products.

What you bring home, in many cases, are the insect eggs, rather than the insects. Unfortunately, they cannot be seen with the naked eye, so go unnoticed, until they hatch into larvae. Even then, in many cases, they are so small you don't notice them until it's too late, and you're infested.

When they hatch, feed, breed, multiply and invade other products, you can become infested before you know it. If you go to the trouble of putting your food products into glass containers, you can contain the spread of these pests - stopping them before they can infest other food products. Notice I said glass. Many of these pests can eat holes in plastic containers, moving easily from one product to another.

They can be killed easily by placing the container in the freezer for three or four days, and then throwing it in the garbage, if you don't care to eat the product.

Never just throw the food away without first killing the insects. Garbage goes to the landfill and those people working there could take some of these insects home on, or in, their clothing. Oops!!...another way of getting infested by these fellows! This way, all you are doing is perpetuating the problem and helping to spread it over a larger area.

Should you discover a package, or box, in one of your cupboards that has been invaded by any of these insects, place the box in the freezer, or burn it, and inspect every other container in the cupboard. If you find any more packages infested, put them in the freezer, or burn also.

Now, remove everything from the cupboard and wash down the entire surface, inside and outside, with a chlorine bleach solution. (One cup per gallon of water.)

Remove the shelves, if possible, and carefully wash the entire surface of every shelf, including the edges. This should be enough to solve your problem, if you do a real good job of cleaning everything, and you're not already infested..

Sometimes, if the infestation has gotten out of hand, you will find larvae hanging from the ceiling or crawling on the walls, counters and table. They look like small maggots with a dark head. If this happens, you are in for a real battle.

At this point, I would wash down the walls, ceiling and every piece of furniture in the kitchen, with a strong disinfecting detergent with some bleach added. My suggestion would be a ½ cup of a good detergent and 1 cup of chlorine bleach in a gallon of hot water.

Make sure you get some of the solution into every crack, nook and cranny, cause that is where they lay some of their eggs. When they can't find a package with a grain or seed product to lay eggs in, they lay then in all of the places mentioned above.

If you don't kill the eggs, the infestation will just start over again when they hatch. Bacillus thuringiensis is nontoxic to humans and kills many of these pests, so if you follow the washing with a good spraying of this product, it will help to solve your problem.

If you have potted plants, or dried flowers, be sure to spray these also, especially the soil in the pots. Many of these pests will lay their eggs in and on these things.

Now that you have resolved your problem with these pests, go to the store where you purchased the product. Alert them of the problem, so they can take the product off the shelves. This will keep others from taking these same pests home and having the troubles you were just involved with. I would suggest you take the product with you to the store, so there isn't any doubt where you purchased it. Also, they should give you back your money, and I believe, some kind of bonus for alerting them before they start losing customers.

FISHY SMELL

When working with fish you will find that upon finishing, your hands smell fishy. You most likely already know that washing your hands with plain soap and water doesn't help at all. Let me tell you how to easily eliminate that fishy odor. Wash your hands as you normally would, then dry them. Now rinse them with a little lemon juice and work it into the skin well. Then wash your hands again with soap and water, and the smell will have vanished. Works great, try it, you will love it.

VOLES

Voles look like fat mice with a short naked tail. These are the creatures that leave the little "U" shaped tunnel you see in the grass, after the snow melts.

They eat seeds, grass roots and that type of stuff, until food gets scarce in the winter, then they will eat the inner bark on shrubs and saplings. This means they gnaw off the outer layer of bark to reach the inner layer. This is the cambium layer and, if they eat it complete around the trunk, the shrub or tree will die. Actually, if they eat too much of the cambium layer, even if they don't eat completely around the trunk, the shrub or tree will die

To stop them from feasting on your stuff, pour cooking oil on the roots and trunks and dust them with hydrated lime. Be generous, and add more when necessary.

A really good way to eliminate these pests during the winter months is to use RO-DEX. This is a seed covered with poison, and they readily eat all they can find, which kills them.

All you need do is make it easy for them to get. Use a section of thin walled sewer pipe, four inches in diameter by twenty four inches long, cap the ends and drill a 1¼" entrance hole in each end cap.

Use this as a bait station, to keep the seed dry and stop birds and other animals from eating the seed. This poison is deadly and will kill any animal that eats it, so be very careful when using it. Always use a bait station, never put this seed out in the open.

Place the bait station under the scrubs, or near the trees you want to protect. Place the bait station under some mulch with just the ends showing. This will make things look natural to the voles and they will quickly go inside to eat the seeds. Check it every five or six days and replenish the seed as needed. Make sure you re-cover the station so everything looks normal again. You can do this all year around if you have a big problem. But remember, the first thing you need to do is make sure you're dealing with VOLES! NOT MOLES!

SQUIRRELS

These fellows can be a really big problem if they get inside your home.
Many of them are social critters and live in family groups, numbering as many as 50 or 60 animals, and sometimes more.
Can you imagine the amount of damage that many rodents can do chewing on the wiring in your house? Yes, they chew constantly because  their teeth never stop growing and they must keep them worn down. Alas, they must chew something that does the job and is easy to chew. Your wiring fits the bill perfectly.

Many of these squirrels are so small that they can fit through a hole an inch, or less, in diameter. If you are troubled with these pests, trapping won't get rid of them, unless you are very good or just plain lucky.

If you resort to poisoning them, and succeed, your home will smell like a sewer for months, because of the number that will die in your walls. Since I no longer hire out to remove these animals, I'll share my secrets with you. The following method was what I used for years and made tons of money with. If you do it right, and don't try cutting corners, you will resolve your problem, and save a lot of money. If you don't, you will have wasted your time and still need to spend lots of money. Here we go.

You need to buy some hardware cloth, this is actually wire screening with ½ holes. Using a 4"X 4" X 24" square post, fold the wire around the post to obtain a 4" square tube, 24" long.

Remove the post and secure the open edges along one side, with some wire to produce a solid walled tunnel. Now cut each corner on one end so you can fold the sides back to form flaps like on a soda cracker box.

These flaps should be approximately 3" to 5" long. (I like them to be 5".) Next you want to cut a piece of the screen approximately 3½" wide by 6" long. That just slips inside the tunnel without catching on the side walls.

This is the door. Slip it inside the box and fastened one end at the top with wire rings, so the door slopes out toward the end opposite the lids, with the bottom 6" away from the open end.

You need the 6" so the door will close behind the squirrel and not rest on his back while he figures out what to do when he finds out he can't go back inside. The top must be fastened so the door moves easily and closes completely without sticking on the sides.

What you have just made is called a "no return". All you have to do now is find the holes where they are going in and out of the house and install the no-return.

To locate the hole or holes, using a ladder, start at one corner of the roof and work your way around the house. Check every crack you see for hairs and shine. The holes they are using will be worn smooth as though they were sand papered.

The edge around the hole will be darker (dirty) than the rest of the area, and may have hair sticking to the sides. You may not see any hole if they are getting in next to a dormer, but check up under the shingles where the dormer and roof meet, in the valley. Sometimes it helps to check dormers from the inside, so that you can tell if they are getting in there. (It's easier to seal dormers from the inside also.)

When you locate the holes, or hole, take the no- return you made and place it over the hole with the lid flaps against the roof or fascia board and staple it in place. (Never put a no-return on the valley of a dormer.)

Now when the squirrels leave, the door will swing up so they can get out, but when they try to get back in the door just closes tighter. Never use more then two no-returns. Seal up any more holes with something the squirrels can't chew through.

You may be forced to leave the no-returns in place permanently, in some locations, especially if your home is in the woods. My advice, if you live close to a woods, is to check each spring and fall to see if any squirrels are chewing new holes in the fascia boards. If they are trying and haven't yet succeeded, just cover the area with some good flashing and paint it.

By the way, squirrels can cut through roll flashing with their claws. Sheet flashing cost more but is thicker and they can't get through it.

If you think you are having a problem with flying squirrels, try to make certain. Once you have identified them, and are sure it's flying squirrels, make ready your no-returns. Don't install them until you have made and hung some good flying squirrel nest boxes in the nearby trees. This gives the squirrels a place to live, and that makes them less likely to try getting back inside your house.

RACCOONS

These critters can be a real pain in the neck, getting into your garbage, into your attic, in your garage, or in your chimney. What they do when they get into your attic, garage or chimney, is live there and  defecate in a corner away from their nest. And that, after a little while, stinks. Now if it's a female, she will usually have pups and raises them in there. Most of the time the female is so quiet that you don't even know she is there, until the pups learn to squawk for her to nurse them. Even then you may not hear them, until they start crawling around up there.

It doesn't take long to realize that one is living in your attic or garage. They are not clean animals - they're filthy critters. No, they are not washing their food when seen putting it in water. They are just wetting it, to make it easier to eat. They have no saliva glands, so their mouth is bone dry. Like I said, it's not long before the odor becomes noticeable, and you realize something is wrong.

If your problem with these fellows is keeping them out of your garbage, try one of these: If you use a plastic garbage can, drill ½" holes spaced every four to six inches around the top of the can about two inches below the lid. Now when you put garbage in the can, always throw in a ½ cup of chlorine bleach on the garbage and the raccoons will stop turning your can over. What happens is they stand on their hind legs and smell at the holes you drilled, smelling the chlorine bleach. This isn't something that smells like food, so they leave. In order to make this work for you, remove the can for several nights. Wash the can throughly with soap and water, before drilling the holes and putting it back out.

However, if you use garbage bags, throw a ½ cup of chlorine bleach in on top of the garbage before you seal the bag and put it out for pick up.

Anytime you have a raccoon in the attic, garage or chimney, you need to call an Animal Damage Control trapper - unless you feel that you can handle this problem yourself, which means you don't need my help, since you already know how to get rid of the animal. Of course, you may just think you know what you are getting into (but you don't). In that case, I would suggest that you definitely should call a professional and forget all of your crazy ideas.

Let me give you some advise: Should you decide that snaring it would be a good idea, you can make a snare by folding a brown extension cord in half and sliding it through a four foot piece of ¾ inch PVC pipe. Make a loop to slip over the animal's head, pull it tight and fold the ends back over the pipe and hold them tight. WHAT NOW??...You say.....I thought you said you knew what you were doing! If you need to ask that question, forget everything I just said and call somebody,

Seriously, you had better have the wife call for some help before the animal eats you for lunch. Next time, be smart....call an expert, before you get into trouble, like I said in the beginning!

The state game department, in most states, license people who operate an Animal Damage Control business and these are the trappers you will need to hire to trap the animal and remove it before it causes a lot of damage.

Yes, your husband can shoot the animal himself, but that isn't always the best way to handle these problems. Sometimes the property owner does more damage getting rid of the pest than the damage caused by the animal.

So before you send "old Dan'l Boone" up to shoot a hole in your roof with his 12 gauge, for the raccoon to escape through, consider hiring a professional. Many times it turns out to be a lot less expensive.

Speaking of expensive, I would suggest you ask for the cost before you hire somebody. Always ask what the quoted price includes. Some Animal Damage Control operators charge you a trip charge, a charge for setting the trap, another charge for catching the animal (even if it's the wrong animal) and still more for disposing of the animal they caught. What you really need to know is what are you being charged for catching and removing the pest animal in question - total cost. Will you be charged for unexpected catches? Like, your problem is with a raccoon living in your attic and, the trapper sets a trap and catches the neighbors cat, or some other animal. Not your fault, you shouldn't be required to pay.

Sometimes there will be several male raccoons living together in your attic. You should be willing to pay for each one caught, or removed. Sometimes it's a female with pups, that should also require an extra charge for removing the pups. Maybe there is a lot of animal defecation that needs removed. Be willing to pay for good service rendered, but try to get information up front so that you know what you are paying for in the end.

DEER

As our population expands more and more into the habitat used by wild animals, they learn to live with us in the habitat we construct for ourselves. This is causing some of us to complain about the problems these animals are making for us.

Usually the main complaint of home owners, concerning deer, is that they eat all of their trees, saplings, shrubs and flowers. This can become very expensive.

There are some pretty good deer repellants being introduced into the market. However, deer are very adaptable creatures.

What you need to do is keep the deer on edge by changing your method or product every two to four weeks. And, you should have at least four different products or methods to use in your rotation.

Say you want to start by spraying with Hot Pepper Wax animal repellant, using a mixture of 10 to 1. After using this for four weeks, the deer are becoming accustomed to it.

Now you add a ½ cup of fish oil to the Hot Pepper Wax animal repellant and you have a brand new product that the deer are not used to. Again, in four weeks you will need to do something else to keep the deer on edge.

This time, you mix in three raw eggs, and you keep them on edge for three or four more weeks. For your last variation, mix in a cup of tea made by soaking some Milorganite fertilizer in cooking oil for a couple of days, and then straining it through a paint strainer or sieve.
All of these mixes are based on the use of one gallon of prepared Hot Pepper Wax.

Of course, you could try hanging some Milorganite fertilizer on stakes around you saplings, trees and shrubs for four weeks. And then changing to Irish Spring soap for another four weeks. Maybe try another brand of smelly soap the next four weeks, etc.

The way you do this is to get some stakes cut to 1½" X 1½" X 4' long. Drive these into the ground around the area you want to protect.

Drive a large finishing nail into the top of the stake, leaving 1½" sticking out.   Get some old nylon stockings and cut them off above the ankle. Tie a knot in the remaining piece and cut it again above the knee. Tie another knot and you end up with three bags. Put two cups of Milorganite in one of the bags and hang it over the nail on the stake.

To use the soap, just drill a hole in the center of the bar and set it on the nail.   With both of these methods, you can keep the deer away for about 12 weeks, before you need to start over again.

Then again, you might just go out and buy some of the deer repellant being sold on the market today. However, if it doesn't work as well as you expected, please remember, I didn't recommend it.

A really great way to keep the deer away is with a good dog, and one of those under ground electric dog fences.   As long as the dog has the run of the place, the deer will not venture onto the property.

Somebody told me that, walking through a horse pasture, they noticed that anywhere the horses had defecated the grass was tall. The horses wouldn't eat there.   Deer, he said, are the same as horses and will not eat around horse manure.

He claims that he uses horse manure spread around his plants and the deer leave everything alone. Try it, it just might work!! Don't forget to let me know the results, so I can pass it along, if it works.

TICKS

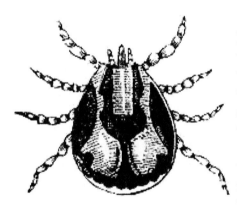

Most people think if they stay away from the woods and the wilder, more remote areas, they can avoid ticks. Think again. You can encounter ticks in the neighborhood park, your back yard, your garden and inside your home, if you have a pet dog or cat.

In recent years the deer tick has been the big issue, because it is a carrier of Lyme disease. However, there are other diseases that are caused by many other ticks, so we should try to stay tick free.

The brown dog tick is found primarily indoors because it likes a drier climate. Ticks have been found on well manicured lawns, in plush neighborhoods, as well as in the woods.

One good way to keep your yard tick free is to have a schedule for spraying the lawn with a good insecticidal soap. In fact, this will keep the lawn pretty much insect free.

Along with the schedule for spraying, you should also have a schedule for inspecting your pet for ticks. The Brown dog ticks, unfed, are about ⅛", while the American dog tick is, unfed, ¼". The deer tick is so small that they are very hard to detect until they fill with blood. In the nymph stage, they are about the size of the period at the end of this sentence.

Now, don't run out and get rid of your dog and/or cat. And, removing all the deer won't help much either. The names don't mean that they are only feeding on these animals, or that the animals are the only carriers of these ticks.

Ticks will feed on just about any mammal they can hitch a ride on, including you and me. When you are giving your little people a bath, be sure to look them over real good for ticks. In fact, a little baby oil rubbed on the tender areas will smother any of the wee little critters that you overlook.

Let's talk about the deer tick that is a carrier of Lyme disease. This particular species lives approximately two years and feed several times during their life cycle. After mating in the fall, the male dies. (Why is it that in the lower life species, the male always dies after mating?)

The female drops off the host animal, lays over 2000 eggs in the soil in the spring, and dies a few weeks later. The larvae hatch after about 30 days, and sometime towards fall they attach themselves to a host, usually a white footed mouse. This is when they get their first meal. After getting a full belly, they drop off, molt and lay up until spring when they emerge as nymphs. Oh boy, second meal coming up, soon as they grab a host.

Since the molt and everything usually takes place in the mouses nest, guess who gets to be the host ....right on, the white footed mouse!

After they have that meal, they lay in wait on the ends of tall grass and shrubs, until someone happens along that they can hitch a ride on. That's when they pass along Lyme disease, if a human is the host.

There has been lots of talk about using Deet for protection against ticks, but my advice is don't put it on your skin. If you can't find something else to use, tuck your pants legs in your socks, and spray your pants and socks.

Recent studies have shown that Deet is able to penetrate the skin and get into the bloodstream. Supposedly, Deet can remain in the skin and fatty tissue for several months.

After reading some articles concerning the possible toxic effects of Deet, I've concluded that I need to find something else to use as a repellent.

By the way, the bacterium that causes Lyme disease is in the blood drawn from the white footed mouse. The white footed mouse is the main reservoir for the bacteria that causes Lyme disease, and the tick's preferred host is the white footed mouse.

The tick feeds once more during the fall or winter, preferably on a deer, finds a female, and we all know what happens then. (Poor fellow).

The problem is that we sometimes get into the chain of this critter's life cycle and become one of the hosts. That's when the tick gets on us, and when it feeds, the bacteria enters our blood and causes Lyme disease. Remember, in the nymph stage this tick is the size of the period here.

It never hurts to take some precautions when you think you might be exposed to ticks. Use a good organic insect repellant, tuck your pants legs into your socks, and remove and wash your clothing when you get home. Don't let the clothes lay around for several days before washing, and use some chlorine bleach in the water.

Tell your husband to lay a plastic tarp on the floor in the trunk of the car before he puts his deer in the trunk to bring home. Have him remove the deer and the tarp from the trunk at the same time. Spray the tarp to kill any ticks that may be on it. Wait awhile, and then hose the tarp off before you fold it up and storage it.

This will get rid of any hitch-hikers that dropped off the deer before they get on you or into your home. Have him hang the deer, and then remove his clothes and hang them outside for several days. It wouldn't hurt if he took a good soapy shower right away too.

Sounds like a lot of trouble for a few ticks, but if one of them gives you Lyme disease, you will learn the hard way that it's best to be sure.

The best way to remove a tick is with fine pointed tweezers. Grasp the tick as close to the skin as possible and gently pull it away from the skin with steady pressure.

Be careful not to pull the tick apart, leaving it's mouth parts in the skin. With the pressure you are applying, the tick will slowly back out. Drop the tick in alcohol and give it to your doctor right away. He can have it checked and find out if it is a carrier of the disease. That way he can give you the vaccination for Lyme Disease, if necessary, possibly warding off the disease. At the very least, since Lyme Disease is difficult to diagnose, he will be able to treat you quickly. This could make it easier to control the disease, or possibly even cure it.

RABBITS

Sometimes when you see the bark on your trees and shrubs roots have been eaten, you blame it on rabbits, and they aren't the real culprits. Rabbits will eat bark as a last resort, but normally can find other things they like better.

However, they will eat most green plants when food is scarce, so when you find your plants being eaten, spray with Hot Pepper Wax at a 16 to 1 ratio. When the bark is being eaten, check under "Voles" in this book.

If you like to keep some of your carrots in the ground for winter and cover them with straw or leaves, you will find that the voles, not rabbits, will eat lots of the carrots - not the tops, the carrots. This is a really good time to use my chipmunk method - it's great for voles. Actually, my chipmunk method works good for any small rodents.

Just remember that rabbits aren't always the culprit, so before you place blame on them, be sure of your facts.

Rabbits can be a real problem in some gardens, depending on the area and how many rabbits there are. The easiest way to solve a rabbit problem in your garden is to fence the garden.

They sell a plastic coated wire fencing with 1" X 2" holes, 24" high. If you install this fencing, it should last for years. I would bend one end over in the shape of the letter L, with the bottom 6" wide. Dig a trench 6" wide, by 6" deep and set the wire into it. Set stakes about every 6' and fill in the trench.

SNAKES

Unfortunately, a lot of people are afraid of snakes, even though you have a better chance of being struck by lightening than being bitten by a poisonous snake.

People that don't go into the wilderness areas of our country probably will live their entire life without ever seeing a poisonous snake, outside of a zoo or a menagerie.

The common snakes you see in your yard are actually working for you; they eat insects and small rodents, keeping the population of these real pests in check. So don't be so quick to kill every snake you see in the garden or yard. Lots of the old farm houses scattered around the country have house snakes, and the people living there rarely ever see a snake in the house; they don't see many mice either!

Usually, the only way they know that there are snakes around is because they find their skins. In order to grow, the snake sheds it's skin and leaves it behind. Many times people tell me that the snakes lay in their driveway. This is because they are reptiles (cold blooded) and their body temperature is regulated by their surroundings. Laying on the warm concrete, or asphalt, warms them up when the temperature is down.

If you have snakes coming into your garage or basement, you can keep them out by using a product called "SNAKE-AWAY".   A rope soaked in kerosene and laid across the opening to the garage will also work - snakes won't crawl over it. Probably the snake followed the scent of some animal, usually a mouse, into the garage or basement, and was looking to make a meal of it, until you interrupted the hunt by killing the snake.

On the other hand, you might prefer to have the snake around rather than the mice it's looking for. In which case, I would suggest you make a hasty retreat so you don't scare the snake away before it catches the mouse.

The best way to keep snakes away from your house, is to make sure that the area is uninviting to the snake. Keep the grass cut short and don't leave any brush piles around the place.

Even when you take all of the precautions, a snake will probably slither by looking for something to eat. To make a very good snake trap; get a 2 inch plastic pipe 2 feet long and an "old fashion" nylon stocking. (or the leg from a panty hose.) Pull about five or six inches of the top band of the stocking over the pipe and rap it tight, then tape it in place with some duct tape.

Be sure the stocking is securely taped to the pipe so the weight of the snake can't pull it off the pipe. Now, to use the trap, set the pipe on a horizontal surface and let the stocking hang down over the edge.

The snake will crawl into the pipe and down into the stocking and can't crawl back out. Works great if you use a mouse nest for bait in the toe of the stocking.

Don't handle the mouse nest with your bare hands; use clean gloves, so the snake doesn't pick up your scent.

Most snakes will try to get away if you give them half a chance. They're more afraid of you than you are of them. You look like a giant to them and they are afraid that you might step on them.

So next time you come across a snake in the yard, walk away and I'll bet the snake will scurry away in the opposite direction, pronto. Most snakes would prefer to never have anything to do with us. Yes, I know you agree, but are afraid. However, don't just kill something simply because you are afraid of it.

MOLES

These critters live under ground and are rarely seen on the surface. If you were to inspect the anatomy of one of these creatures, you would see why they don't run around above ground - they can't run, because of the way they are built. Sometimes your cat will catch one. Believe me, the cat heard the mole tunneling under the grass, watched the progress and finally scooped the mole up with some of the grass, then killed the mole because it couldn't move fast enough to get away back under the sod.

Many people ask me why the moles are tunneling under the grass; the reason is, that's where dinner is being served. Moles love to eat grubs and grubs love to eat grass roots, so the grubs move in to feast on the grass roots and the moles come to feast on the grubs.

Certainly, moles eat other things, such as worms and other insect larvae, but the grubs are the easiest to get throughout the spring and summer months because they stay just under the grass, in the roots. And I believe the moles like the taste of grubs better than the other items on their menu.

As the ground starts to freeze in the fall, forcing the grubs to move deeper into the soil to become dormant, you see less tunneling in the yard. However, this is when you start seeing the piles of dirt in the yard, called push ups.

These are caused by the moles pushing the dirt from their tunnels to the surface. When the moles go deeper into the soil, they haven't any choice but to push the dirt up to the surface, every-so-often, while tunneling. But as soon as the ground thaws out, the grubs move back up under the grass roots and the moles follow them.

Make certain you are dealing with moles not voles, that's important if you expect results.

It you want to drive the moles away temporally, try some Hot Pepper Wax Brand "Mole and Gopher Chase"- it works great. Of course, they will return eventually, so for a more permanent solution use Milky Spore - it lasts up to 20 years. In fact, at my place it lasted for 23 years. I sold the place then, so I don't know if it lasted any longer.

Milky Spore is a bacillus, or bacteria, that attacks the grubs of the Japanese and May Beetles, and some other scarab beetles. Milky Spore is harmless to humans and pets; in fact, it doesn't even affect the adult beetles, just the larvae(grubs). You can apply Milky Spore to your lawn in the spring, or late summer, when the temperature at night is above fifty degrees.

MILDEW

If you have mildew appearing on your walls, this normally means that there is, or was, a leak, and moisture is the cause of the mildew. Another problem that is a cause of mildew is poor ventilation. In any case, you must locate the cause and correct it.

Mildew is a fungus, and if you just paint over it with a regular paint, it will eventually start showing up on the surface again.

There are paints that have fungicide in them that will kill the mildew and stop it from surfacing again. However, if you want to use regular paint, I have a formula that can help you.

To kill the mildew on the wall before you re-paint with a regular paint, wash the wall with the following mixture.

> ½ cup of trisodium phosphate
> ¼ cup Tide laundry detergent
> 1 qt. chlorine bleach
> 3 qts. warm water

Mix the ingredients in a bucket and scrub the wall with a brush, then rinse thoroughly with clean water. BE SURE YOU ARE WEARING RUBBER GLOVES WHENEVER HANDLING ANYTHING WITH TRISODIUM PHOSPHATE IN IT - IT'S CAUSTIC. WOULDN'T HURT TO PROTECT YOUR EYES EITHER!

Mildew in clothing presents a little different problem. If you find that some of your packed away clothing has become mildewed, sort the clothing. Anything that must be dry cleaned should immediately be taken to the dry cleaners. Be sure to inform them of the mildew problem. Clothing that can be washed should be soaked in X O Concentrate before being washed with a mild laundry soap.

If your problem is a mildewed rug or carpeting, spray it throughly with X O Concentrate and allow it to air dry. It may take several applications to get the mildew completely out of the rug or carpet. It's important that you find the cause of the mildew and eliminate it so the problem doesn't come back. Removing the stain and odor from a rug or carpet doesn't cure the problem. You must find the cause of the mildew and correct the cause before the problem is solved.

CONCRETE

To clean badly soiled concrete, begin by repairing all of the defects, cracks, etc. Let the repairs dry and setup for a week. Make a cleaning paste by mixing one part of Portland cement to 1¼ parts of a very fine sand. Add enough water to make a thick paste, similar to pancake batter. Apply with a brush and immediately scour with a wooden float. Keep the area damp until completely finished.

When finished, allow to set for an hour and then remove the excess with a trowel. When completely dry (usually the next day) rub down with a burlap rag to complete the job. Your job will have a better appearance if you complete the burlap rubbing without stopping.

Another way to clean concrete is to wash with the muriatic acid sold in most paint stores. The acid is usually mixed with an equal amount of water and brushed into the concrete. Rinse with clear water.

Always wear rubber gloves and eye protection when working with acid of any kind.

To give concrete a hard surface, use the following:

> ¼ oz. sulfuric acid (battery acid)
> 3 lbs. zinc sulfate
> 2 gallons of water

Stir the acid into the water, being careful not to splash any on yourself, then stir in the zinc sulfate and keep stirring until completely dissolved.

Apply a coat to the concrete and allow it to work for four hours. Then brush the surface with water and mop dry. Next apply a second coat and let it dry. The surface will now be hardened.

To repair a crack in concrete, thoroughly clean the area and roughen the crack with a chisel. Then go over the area with a wire brush and vacuum up the dust and loose particles. Wet the surface of the area and the crack thoroughly, but don't leave any water puddles on the surface.

Make a thick creamy mixture of patching cement and brush it into the crack. Before this dries, fill the crack completely with a stiff mixture of patching cement. Tamp the cement into the cavity and smooth with a wooden float. When the cement starts to harden, finish with a steel float.

Keep the patch damp for several hours by laying a damp rag over the repair.

With larger cracks, you can use some pea gravel in your mix.

To color concrete, add dye when mixing it. The cement will always dry lighter than it looks when wet, so you may want to add more dye. Never paint concrete with latex paint - it only covers the surface and peels off. Use a good oil base paint and thin it by mixing equal parts of the paint and the paint thinner. Then apply several coats, allowing each to soak into the concrete before applying the next one. This way the cement will retain the color as it wears from walking on it, instead of the paint wearing off in patches.

With some paints, you may need to use more thinner to get the paint to the consistency of water, so it soaks into the concrete properly. They say that vinyl cleaner/wax does an excellent job of sealing concrete. Just apply and let it soak in and dry, and you are done.

I like to treat new concrete with a mixture of one part boiled linseed oil to three parts terpentine, for the first coat. After allowing it to dry for several days, I use a fifty/fifty mixture of the same ingredients. I find this to hold up better that many of the costly commercial products available.

SILVERWARE

If you have good silverware and it is tarnished, try this method to clean it up. Use an aluminum baking pan 9" X 13". Dissolve a tablespoon of trisodium phosphate in a quart of boiling water in a stainless steel pot.

Put your silverware in the baking pan and cover with the mixture. Allow the silverware to soak for several minutes, then remove it and rinse the silverware with clean warm water. You will need to lightly buff the silverware with a soft cloth to have it shine real bright. Be sure to clean the baking pan right away - trisodium phosphate is corrosive.

Another good way to clean silver is to soak the silver in water that you boiled potatoes in. Soak the silver for several hours, then rinse and polish with a soft cloth.

A quick polish can be made using caulk and ammonia. Mix to a soft paste, rub the silver with a soft cloth dipped in the paste, rinse and dry. Do this in a well ventilated area.

Or, you can make a liquid polish using 4 ounces of whiting, 2 ounces of Ivory soap flakes, ¼ ounce of household ammonia and 16 ounces of water. Heat the water to dissolve the soap.

When the soap is dissolved, mix in whiting and allow the mixture to cool. When cooled to room temperature, add the ammonia. Keep tightly capped and shake well before using.

A good furniture or floor polish will keep silver from tarnishing. Storing your silver in a polyethylene freezer bag will keep it from tarnishing also.

A quick dip cleaner for silverware can be made as follows:

> Place some Reynolds Wrap aluminum strips in a large plastic bowl. Place your silverware on the strips and then cover the silverware with boiling water and add 3 or 4 tablespoons of baking soda. Allow the silverware to soak for 15 minutes or so, remove, dry and polish with a soft cloth.

A non-tarnishing storage bag can be made by soaking some flannel material in a solution of 1 ounce of zinc acetate dissolved in a pint of water. Squeeze out the excess solution and allow the cloth to dry. Sew into a bag and store your silverware tarnish free. Always wash the silverware before using.

ROSES

Through out the years, people have asked me many questions about roses. Like how do I prepare them for winter? Good question, but hard to give a general answer to.

Strong winter winds can break off shoots or loosen the roots, so maybe you better shorten them some. Roses need protected in cold winters. In poorly drained soils water freezes, and lifts and breaks the roots, causing damage.

It might be advisable to mound up the soil and/or place some straw or leaves a foot deep loosely over the cut-back roses. The straw, or leaves, can be held in place with chicken wire. Or maybe you would rather stake the canes instead of cutting them off. You could still use the straw or leaves for protection from the cold. Climbing roses should definitely be tied to prevent wind damage.

Stop feeding nitrogen fertilizers in the fall - use super phosphate and kelp to help them harden off for winter. Of course, some roses are hardy, some are not so hardy. You must know what type you have.

Pruning roses isn't hard, just remember to cut the shoots cleanly, at an angle above a bud that faces in the direction you want the shoot to grow. Remove all of the dead canes at ground level

At this time, remove all of the damaged or diseased canes, back to healthy wood, that looks like a green apple. Remove thin shoots, smaller than a pencil; they usually produce poor blooms.

Prune everything else back by one third, unless you know what type of rose you are dealing with, in which case you can prune accordingly.

Many ask what deadheading is. Deadheading is removing the faded flowers in order to stimulate new young shoots, and further blooming throughout the season.

A lot of people ask about moving roses. Well, I wouldn't move roses older than two or three years old. They usually don't do well if moved after that age.

Roses are susceptible to a number of diseases, such as black spot, which most likely occurs under warm moist conditions. Left unchecked, it could defoliate the plant. To prevent this, mulch the plants, pick off and pick up all effected leaves.

Water early in the day so the leaves can dry before evening, or be very careful not to wet the leaves. Black Spot usually occurs during warm moist conditions. If left unchecked, black spot can completely destroy a plant.

To help control black spot, dissolve a teaspoon of baking soda in a quart of warm water and throughly spray the infected plants. For a severe infection, use a sulfur spray, applied weekly. Remove all diseased leaves and pick up any that fall of their own accord.

Powdery mildew is another serious disease for some roses. A powdery grey deposit forms on younger leaves then on older leaves and buds, and sometimes spreads to the canes. At the first sign of this disease, pick off all affected parts and start a weekly spraying with sulfur.

Canker sometimes attacks roses. Should you ever have this problem, the best approach is to prune off all effected parts of the plant.

Rust is a problem in some areas, and is manifested by reddish orange bubbles appearing on the under sides of the leaves. At the first sign of this disease, pick off the infected parts. Where this disease is common, start in the spring spraying with sulfur, weekly.

Viral diseases are usually spread by feeding insects, so control the insects to control this problem. And, of course, there are loads of insects that just love to eat your roses - like Aphids.

Several types of aphids attack roses, and I like to control these with insecticidal soap, Hot Pepper Wax Insect Repellant, Rotenone Pyrethrin, Sabadilla or Nicotine.

Japanese Beetles can be controlled with insecticidal soap, rotenone, pyrethrin or BTK.

Thrips can be controlled with insecticidal soap, neem, rotenone, pyrethrin, ryania, sabadilla or diatomaceous earth.

Spider mites can be controlled with insecticidal soap, rotenone, pyrethrin or neem.

Rose Chafer can be controlled with rotenone, or pyrethrin.

Rose Curculios can be controlled with rotenone, or pyrethrin.

These, I believe, are the common insects that attack roses and other plants.

So, you're going to plant some bare root roses, Well, let me give you some pointers. About an hour before you intend to plant the roses, put them in a bucket of water to soak. Dig your hole 18 inches deep and 18 inches in diameter.

Mix approximately a quart of aged manure with the dirt you took from the hole and make a mound in the bottom of the hole.

Put the rose on the mound, making sure the union is 2 inches under the surface, if you live where the temperature drops to 20° or less, otherwise keep it at, or just above, the surface. Next fill in the hole, firming the soil as you go. Then form a dam 2 inches high around the rose and fill it with water.

After the water soaks in, form a dome 6 inches high around the rose to keep the stem from drying out while the rose gets rooted. As the leaves open, gradually remove the excess soil.

BIRDS

Birds occasionally cause problems by roosting in buildings where there are openings and roof trusts. These birds are usually English Sparrows, Pigeons, Grackles, or some other trash birds.

This problem can be eliminated, many times, by hanging 1¼" wide strips of black plastic garbage bags from the trusts.

As the birds come to roost, their wings make the plastic wave and this scares the birds away. A better way, I believe, is to trap the birds and destroy them.

You can buy a good sparrow trap that will catch and hold up to 30 birds at a time.

There is also a caulk that you can spread on the trusts that birds will not land on or walk in.

Another problem people have is from woodpeckers digging holes in the side of their homes. This is sometimes caused by a vibration that woodpeckers think is an insect under the siding. And, of course, sometimes there are insects under the siding. If you are having this problem, use a stethoscope to listen for any sounds you might hear. If you don't have a stethoscope, place a glass up against the wall they are digging in and put your ear to the bottom of the glass.

You should be able to hear a hum, provided the problem is not insects. If you can hear something, try to locate what is causing the sound and stop it. If you can do this, you will correct the problem. The woodpecker should leave then. If you can't locate the source of the sound, or can't be bothered looking, just staple some strips as described below.

Drive a 16 penny nail in each edge of the wall and tie a piece of binder twine between the nails. Cut a plastic leaf bag into 1" strips, attached at the bottom. Place these over the twine at 6" intervals and cover with a small piece of cardboard. Then staple them in place, through the cardboard. Now, if you did everything right, the strips will flutter every time the bird approaches, causing it to think a predator is after it. The bird will leave immediately and not return for awhile. Do not remove the twine until the bird has stayed away for at least 2 weeks. Otherwise, you may be forced to put it back up.

In the spring of the year, during mating season, the male woodpeckers drum on, whatever, to entice females to stop by and possibly become their mate. It may be that he likes the sounds coming from your wall. Again, use the plastic strips.

If you feed the birds, and lots of us do, you should have some idea which birds eat what. Following is a list. Check it out before you buy bird seed.

Just about all seed eaters eat Black Oiled Sunflower Seeds, or Hulled Sunflower Seeds. Cardinals, Grosbeaks, Jays, Chickadees, Titmice and Nuthatches love Striped Sunflower Seeds.

White Throated Sparrows, Cardinals, House Finches, Titmice and Morning Doves all eat Safflower Seeds.

Thistle Seeds are eaten by Finches, Sparrows and Morning Doves.

Woodpeckers, Titmice, Jays, Nuthatches and Chickadees all eat Nut Meats.

Red and White Millet is eaten by Juncos, Morning Doves and Cardinals.

Cracked Corn is eaten by Morning Doves and some Sparrows.

Goldfinches, Juncos, Titmice, Jays, Chickadees and Sparrows all like Peanut Pieces.

Peanut Butter is eaten by Robins, Creepers, Titmice Chickadees and Woodpeckers.

Orange halves are eaten by Orioles, Woodpeckers and Warblers.

Suet is liked by just about all birds in the winter, especially when mixed with seeds, nut pieces, etc.

Robins, Wrens and Bluebirds like Currents, Raisins, Grapes and Cherries.

Just about all backyard birds love Mealworms, especially Bluebirds.

If you feed the birds during the winter, be sure to give them a good source of fat, usually in the form of suet, with a good selection of grains and seeds.

It's a good idea to add some grit to your bird feeding program. Birds need grit to grind their food - no teeth.

Peanut butter is a good source of high protein food, especially when mixed with suet and seeds.

If you feed baked goods, be careful, they become moldy quickly, and can cause disease. Always pick up any baked goods the birds don't eat, or just put out enough so that the birds finish it all. My own preference for baked goods is to allow them to get stale and hard. It will last longer and be less likely to get moldy.

And again, putting out small amounts, and letting the birds finish it, is better than throwing out a large amount that sits until some of it gets moldy and kills some of your birds.

Let me give you some good suet mixes:

High Protein Suet Mix:

> 3 cups of suet
> ½ cup of stale bread or baked goods in
>   crumbs
> ½ cup Hulled Sunflower Seeds
> ¼ cup of White Proso Millet
> ½ cup of ground meat

Melt the suet in a pan and set aside to thicken a little. Mix everything else together in a bowl and add the suet when thick enough to mix. Mix well, pour into your mold and when completely cool, feed the birds.

How about another high protein mix:

> 1 cup of suet
> 1 cup chunky peanut butter
> ½ cup of cornmeal
> ½ cup whole wheat flour
> 1 cup fine cracked corn
> ½ cup hulled sunflower seeds

Melt the suet and add the peanut butter, stirring until throughly mixed and blended together. Mix the other ingredients in a bowl, and when the suet/peanut butter mix is cool, mix together into a dough, and it is ready to use.

Snack Bar Mix:

> ¾ pound of ground suet
> ¼ cup chopped peanuts
> ½ cup raisins
> ¼ cup cooked oatmeal
> ¼ cup cooked rice
> ¼ cup fine cracked corn
> ¼ cup hulled sunflower seeds

Mix everything together in a bowl, except the suet. Melt the suet and allow it to cool until thickened. Add the suet to the other ingredients and pour everything into your molds to cool, and then feed all the birds.

You say that you're just starting out and need to know how to attract birds to your feeder. That's not so hard to do. Just put your feeder out in late August, or early September, and fill it with a good mixture of bird seed, or just use oiled sunflower seeds, if you wish. Most birds like to eat the oiled sunflower seeds.

Now get some stale bread, break it up into small pieces and throw it under the feeder and wait for the birds to come to the feast. One caution: never allow your feeder to stay empty for more that half a day. If you do, the birds may find another place to eat and not return.

It's a good idea to include some suet, or suet mix, in your daily feeding program during the winter - helps the birds to keep warm. Be sure to stop feeding suet to the birds when the young are in the nests. It's very hard for young birds to shallow and could smother them when the mother bird stuffs it down their throats.

During the winter, it's very important that you set out water for the birds to drink. One of my listeners suggested that if you have an old crock pot - this works great. I haven't tried this, so if you do, let me know how it works for you.

Another good way to keep the water from freezing is to use a heated dog watering dish. I use one of these for my own dog every winter and frequently see lots of birds sitting around the edge of the bowl getting a drink

One man told me that he puts warm water out and just drops a hot stone in it every hour or so. He keeps several stones in a pot on the stove, and every time he puts out a hot one he returns the cold one to the pot on the stove. Sounds like that might work, if you don't mind going to all that trouble.

It really doesn't matter how you do it, as long as you do. Feeding our little feathered friends all winter is really great. But, if you don't have some way for them to get a drink occasionally, you might not see many birds at your feeder.

WINTER BULB GARDEN

Instead of storing your bulbs all winter, why not enjoy the beauty of your flowers during the winter? You can, by following a few simple steps. Force spring blooming bulbs to flower during the winter. The best bulbs to try this with are Crocus, Daffodils, Hyacinths and Tulips.

Almost every hardy bulb can be forced, but not all of them will flower indoors. If you have other bulbs, give them a try, you might be surprised with the results you get. Make sure all the bulbs you plan to force are plump, solid and don't have any blemishes. Use the biggest bulbs you have and don't buy cheap stuff if you want good looking flowers. Here's how you go about forcing bulbs.

Get some containers with a drain hole in the bottom. If there isn't a drainage hole in the bottom, don't use it. Only containers that are twice as tall, or taller, than your bulbs should be used. This is necessary for good root growth. If you are using new clay pots, put them in a bucket of water to soak for at least one day before using them.

The best soil is loose and crumbly, like a good loam. If you can make a hard ball of your soil, it has too much clay in it. Add some sand or peat moss to correct the problem.

Don't use the soil from where you were growing bulbs before - get new soil elsewhere. Be sure the soil is free of manure and fertilizer. I would suggest you mix your own soil by mixing one part good soil, one part peat moss and one part sand.

Next we need to pot the bulbs. First put a small stone over the drainage hole so the water can get out, but the soil can't. (You might want to look under potting plants for better ways to plug the hole.) Next put enough soil in the pot so that the top of the bulbs just reach the edge of the pot.

Gently press the bulbs into the soil close enough to each other so that they almost touch. Use as many bulbs as you can get into the pot comfortably. Now fill the pot with soil around the bulbs and firm it down gently, but don't pack it. Only the very tips of the bulbs should be above the soil.

Place each completed pot in a pan of water and soak it until the surface of the soil is moist. It would be a good idea to number each pot with a marking pen, that way you can have a paper that corresponds with the numbers, telling you what is in each pot and when you planted them, including the colors and varieties.

Winter cold is necessary for spring flowering bulbs to develop a good root system; usually 12 to 16 weeks is required, depending on the variety of the bulb. You can provide this by using an outdoor rooting bed, or by placing the pots indoors in a cold area.

The easiest method for rooting bulbs is also the most desirable - a cold dark location under cover - like your basement, garage or maybe a shed near the house. Whatever location you use, the temperature must be maintained between 40 - 50 degrees.

Above or below these temperatures is not going to work well, or possibly not at all. If you keep the pots inside, be sure to water them regularly to have good results. Remember, NO LIGHT, keep the pots in the dark.

After your cold period, the bulbs should have a good root system and are ready for forcing. Check the pots. The roots should be coming out the drainage holes. If the roots aren't visible, turn the pot over and tap it to remove the contents so you can see if the root system is well developed.

If things don't look good, return the pot to the dark and wait another two weeks or so. Check every two weeks until the roots fill the bottom of the pot.

When you feel that the roots are developed enough, place the pot in a semi-dark location in the house. Make sure it's not too hot for the pot - no more than 60 degrees. After the pots are used to their new environment, about a week, place them in a room with normal temperatures - not above 72 degrees. They need light, but not direct sunlight, and don't set them near a heat source. Enjoy your efforts, and your indoor bulb flower garden!!

JAPANESE BEETLES

This particular insect is probably one of the most destructive insects we have to deal with. As an adult, it devastates many trees, shrubs, flowers and food crops. In fact, they feed on almost 300 kinds of plants.

When the adult beetles are feeding on leaves, they usually skeletonize them, leaving large, irregular holes in the leaves.

If the infestation is heavy, they can destroy most of the leaves on whatever they are eating. They love ripening fruit and will eat until nothing edible is left.

They can cause farmers big problems when they move into a corn field. They gobble up the silk as fast as it grows, keeping the kernels from forming.

The adult beetle is about ⅜ inch long and has a green/bronze shiny body covering. Males and females look alike, but the male is normally smaller.

The adults appear around the beginning of summer, or in late spring, on their favorite plants - depending on the area. They will be very active for 6 weeks or so, and then gradually disappear. They only fly in the daytime and are very active on warm sunny days, moving quickly about from plant to plant. Every so often the female will go to the ground to borrow down, in approximately 2 inches or so, and lay some eggs, then return to feeding. By midsummer the eggs hatch and the young grubs start feeding on the grass roots.

As cold weather moves in the grubs borrow deeper into the ground where they remain inactive all winter. In early spring they return to feed on the roots again, until late spring. They change into pupae at this time and in approximately two weeks they emerge from the ground as adult beetles. Their life cycle takes one year.

In addition to all the problems the larvae and adult beetles cause, moles, skunks and raccoons have found the grubs very tasty and will destroy a lawn digging them up for dinner.

The thing about this that bothers me is that this beetle is native to Japan. Back around 1916, they discovered some of these beetles some place in New Jersey, (seems that they snuck in on some plants that were imported from that country). And the rest of the story, you are well aware of.

Everybody wants to know how to get rid of these problems, and there are lots of people with lots of ideas. I would suggest that the best solution to all of the problems would be to get rid of the beetles. The way to do that, in my opinion, is to use Milky Spore.

This product is a disease that only attacks the larvae of the beetles. It doesn't even have any effect on the adult beetles. It's not harmful to us, our pets, birds or animals, it only effects the beetle larvae - the GRUBS. Kill the grubs and you destroy the beetles. That stops the moles, skunks and raccoons from destroying the lawns. And, of course, no beetles, no plants being destroyed!

POTTING PLANTS

Here's a tip for you folks that pot plants to keep all year around. Ever notice that the stone you placed in the bottom of a clay pot, before you put the soil in, sealed the hole and water had a hard time getting out? Well, this tip will solve that problem for you! Just roll up some nylon stocking into a ball, slightly bigger than the hole in the pot. Force it firmly into the hole and use a piece of copper wire to keep it from going all the way through. No soil can get out and the water runs out like nothing was there at all. In big pots with large holes, you can put some sphagnum moss in the nylon.

A good source for the copper wire is Romex house wiring. When you see a new house being built, ask the electrician for a small piece of number 14 Romex. A 12 inch piece of Romex has three thin copper wires in it, when cut to 2 inch pieces, this gives you enough to do 18 pots.

Another way to let water out of your clay pots, without losing the soil, is to cut a piece of fiberglass window screening to fit the bottom of your pot. After fitting it into the bottom of the pot, put an inch or so of pea gravel on top of it, and then cover the pea gravel with a snug fitting piece of nylon stocking to keep the soil from getting out. Take your pick, either way works great.

PEPPERMINT OIL

This is a great item to use for repelling mice, and other rodents, when you need to store a car, motor home, trailer or whatever. What you do is put a small ball of cotton into the lid from a soda bottle and place some peppermint oil on the cotton. You will need plenty of these to take care of an auto, etc., so make lots.

Place enough caps under the hood, under the seats, under the dashboard and in the trunk, to make everything smell strongly of peppermint.

Remember, there is no such thing as too much in this case. The stronger the smell the better it works. In fact, with builders plastic sheeting, you can, with a little "Yankee Ingenuity," completely wrap the automobile with the peppermint oil inside. Crazy??

Think of it this way - a roll of builders plastic sheeting, when rolled out and opened is 10 feet wide and 100 feet long. Say the auto is 20 feet long, 4 feet high and 6 feet wide - you set 2 strips of plastic, 50 feet long on the garage floor and tape them together with duct tape. You now have a sheet 20 feet wide by 50 feet long.

Put your peppermint oil caps inside the automobile as described, then place some under the automobile, all around the outer edge. Caps under the automobile should be spaced approximately 6 to 8 inches apart.

Fold the plastic up over the hood of the automobile, then holding it in place, have someone fold the other end up over the trunk and tape them together.

Pick up one side and tape it securely to the top side of plastic that is hanging down - then do the other side the same way. Now if you were careful and did a good folding and taping job, your automobile is securely wrapped with enough peppermint oil inside to keep it safe all winter.

Be sure you check occasionally for holes, mice will sometimes chew a hole and then leave. Holes will let the odor out and cause the repellant effect to dissipate quickly. When you find a hole, duct tape it shut.

When spring comes and you want to use the automobile, simply unwrap it, pull it out of the garage and open the doors, hood and trunk, and remove all of the soda bottle caps. Let the car set with everything open for awhile. In several hours the odor will be so weak that you will not mind driving the automobile.

However, if you really feel that you want to eliminate all of the peppermint oil odor from the automobile, just spray the interior with some X O Concentrate.

XO CONCENTRATE

This product is an odor digester that really works great. Once you have tried it you will never be without a bottle. You should be able to purchase a bottle from any good hardware store, pet supply store or farm supply store. If not, have the store call the distributor at 1-800-344-6668 and order some for you.

MICE

Many times you store something in boxes, etc, and then later when you open the box you find that mice have defiled the contents.

Or maybe you put the lawn tractor, lawn mower, garden tiller, or whatever, away for the winter and in the spring found that mice had chewed the wiring, to the tune of big bucks! You can solve this type of problem with peppermint oil.

Soak some cotton in peppermint oil and place the cotton inside of a small plastic medicine vial, that you have drilled lots of holes in. Before you pack the box, set several of these vials in the bottom.

Seal the box with packing tape to keep the odor inside and when you open it, everything will be in good shape - smelling like peppermint oil. It wouldn't hurt to check the box every so often for holes. If you find a hole, check to see if you can smell the oil coming out of the hole. If not, re-oil the vials.

Air the items out to get rid of the peppermint odor. You can use peppermint oil to keep mice out of anything that you can close up - like draws, closets, trunks, etc. One man uses it successfully to keep his mountain cabin mice and squirrel free, and claims that he hasn't seen either inside since he started using the peppermint oil.

Check elsewhere in this book, under peppermint oil, for instructions on how to store large items like your automobile, trailer or mobile home. With a little work, just about anything can be protected from mice damage.

Sometimes you just want to catch the mice, and if that is your goal, be sure to read "Mouse Traps" in this book. There are several good ideas there for making traps at home. Of course, you could just buy a mouse trap, if you don't wish to make one.

PRUNING

In order to do a good job when pruning, you must know something about plant growth and flower production, especially for the plant you intend to prune. Growth is through the buds, terminal and lateral.

Growth is normally through the terminal buds. However, if it is injured, faulty or removed, then the immediate lateral bud will take over.

Now, when pruning, you must look at the entire tree, shrub or bush. Decide how you want it to look when you have finished pruning it, and it has grown through the lateral bud on the limb you pruned.

Pruning removes the terminal bud, and you must decide before you start to cut the limb which lateral bud you want to continue the growth of that limb. Look closely at the limb and decide what direction you want the limb to continue to grow in. Pick the lateral bud that is closest to that direction and make your cut ⅛ to ¼ inch in front of the bud, giving it a chance to survive and take over the growth of that limb.

During pruning, you should remove all dead wood, along with all of the excess growth (water sprouts) and any limbs that are rubbing each other.

The object of pruning is to shape the plant, help it to gain better growth, and to maximize the production of flowers and fruits. Pruning also helps the plant to live longer, when done properly.

Pruning always causes wounds - unfortunately, a necessary evil. All wounds on a plant must be considered serious. These are sore spots on the plant and until it has healed, it is constantly subject to fungi.

Fungi spore are always present in the atmosphere and when they land on an open wound, they vegetate, and through rapid development, cause a diseased condition. You should be careful of breaking or rubbing the bark of plants with equipment for this reason.

I always start pruning my trees and shrubs by removing all of the dead wood. Next I remove all of the water suckers. Then and only then, I step back and try to visualize how the plant should look, after it has been pruned and regrown. Usually, when my trees are to be pruned, I take several days to look and think before I make my first cut. Remember, a little pruning is much better than excessive pruning.

Some shrubs flower on year old wood and should be pruned after blooming. Others bloom on new wood and should be pruned when dormant. Before you start pruning any of your shrubs, be sure you know when they bloom or you may not have flowers next season.

PILOT LITE

Next time you need to light a pilot lite that is hard to reach with a regular match, use a piece of dry spaghetti. Just light the end and use the slow burning spaghetti to reach the hard to get at pilot. Works great, if you remember to keep some thin spaghetti handy instead of always using rigatoni.

HUMIDIFIER

Having problems with lime deposits forming in your humidifier? Just drop in a couple of aspirin tablets in the tank each time you fill it, and no more lime deposits. House smelling kind of funky? A small amount of your favorite spice dropped into the water will give off a nice aroma. Cologne also works.

SAVING HOT WATER

Next time you cook a roast in the oven for supper, put a large pot of water in the oven when you remove the roast and close the door. By the time you finish eating, the water will be just right for doing the dishes.

TEAKETTLE

Keep a couple of glass marbles in your teakettle to keep hard water deposits from building up. Every time you boil water, the marbles will be jumping around inside the pot, keeping it clean. If you already have a build up in your kettle, just put a half cup of vinegar in the kettle, fill it with water and allow it to boil for 3 or 4 minutes. Then dump out the water and the scum will go with it.

PLYWOOD SHEETS

When you are alone and need to carry a 4X8 sheet of plywood, do this. Take a piece of rope approx. 18 feet long and tie the ends together forming a loop. Then hook the loop around two corners of the sheet of plywood. Grab the doubled rope in the center and off you go - holding the top edge of the plywood for balance. No problem at all, provided you are more than four feet tall.

PAINTING & STAINING

To keep your paint or stain from running down the sides of the can when you wipe the brush on the container's edge, punch holes in the bottom of the grove that the lid sets in. This way, the excess paint will drip back into the can, instead of running down the sides. When you finish painting or staining and need to store what you have left, seal the can and store it, by setting it on it's lid. That way any scum coat that forms will be on the bottom of the can when you open it, instead of on the top.

TIED TIGHT

Use damp twine to tie your package and when the string dries it will be tighter than you could ever make it. Just remember to use cotton twine, not nylon or plastic.

CLEAN OVEN

Have a dirty oven that needs cleaned? Place a bowl of ammonia in the oven and let it set overnight with the door closed. In the morning, or when you are going to do the cleaning, open the door and step back immediately to allow the fumes to dissipate. After several moments have passed, and the fumes have dissipated, you can easily clean the oven with plain soap and hot water.

KEEP IT FRESH

An apple cut in half and placed inside an airtight container with either bread or bakes goods will keep them moist, and fresh for several days.

BLACK WALNUTS

Black walnuts will come out of the shell in much larger pieces if you soak the nuts in boiling water for 35 to 45 minutes before cracking them. Another good method for cracking most nuts, is to pre-heat the oven to 275°. Heat the nuts on a cookie sheet for twenty minutes. Remove them from the oven and allow them to cool before cracking them.

PAINTING CLEAN

Going to do some painting, don't want to keep moving newspaper around to set your paint can on? That's okay, just use your hot glue gun to glue a paper plate to the bottom of the can before you open it. If you are going to use a Styrofoam plate, don't use hot glue.

EASY HAULER

Always seem to be hauling things on top of your car and don't have a roof rack? Don't want to scratch the finish? Just carry one of those camping mattresses, that you blow up by mouth, in your trunk. You will always be ready to haul things without worrying about the finish on your automobile. Just blow it up and set it on top of the car roof. Place whatever you are hauling on top of the mattress and tie it down.

Speaking of tying it down. You will have an easier time tying things on your car if you have some rope and several bungie cords. These will also help to keep the load tied tight when traveling. Hook the bungie under the car and attach the rope to the other end. Now go over the load and hook another bungie under the opposite side of the car. Put the rope through the S hook and pull it tight; tie it securely. Do this several times to hold the load down.

INK STAINS

Some ink stains can be removed from clothing by applying a paste of dry mustard and water. Let set for a few minutes before washing.

PAINT STAINS

Some oil based paint spots can be removed from clothing by applying a mixture of equal parts of turpentine and ammonia to the spot.

SWEAT STAINS

Human sweat can be removed from clothing by dampening the spot and sprinkling heavily with Twenty Mule Team Borax. Roll up the clothing and allow to set for 15 minutes, then rinse with cold water and the stain will be gone.

ROAD TAR SPOTS

When you get road tar on your automobile, it' very hard to remove, unless you first soak the spot with boiled linseed oil. After a few minutes, the tar will rub right off with a rough cloth.

CLEAN WASHER

You can keep your washing machine clean, and smelling good, if you set the water level at low, add a half gallon of white vinegar and let it go through the wash cycle only, and drain. Refill on low and add another half gallon of the vinegar and let the washer complete it's cycle.

When it shuts off, take a sniff and you will be pleased. Do this whenever you start to smell that old funky odor in the washer tub.

WOODEN BOWL

Wooden salad bowls and cutting boards will last longer, and look much better, if you apply some olive oil on them, every now and then. Allow the oil to set overnight, then wipe off and buff with a soft cloth.

BLUE JEANS

Want to keep the dark blue color in you jeans a lot longer? If so, soak the jeans in a tub of cold, clear water for 5 minutes, then add a cup of table salt and stir, or agitate, to dissolve the salt. Allow to set for 15 minutes, rinse with clear water, dry and enjoy.

WALL SPOT CLEANER

Art-gum erasers work great for removing dirty marks from painted or wallpapered walls.

CAR TIP

In the winter keep about 6 or 8 asphalt shingles in your automobile. Then if you get stuck in the snow or ice, it's easy to lay a row of shingles under your drive wheel and out you go. Remember to pick up your shingles, you may need them again before you get home.

SPLINTERS

Got a splinter - can't see it? · Just coat the area with iodine and the wood will absorb the iodine, and no problem seeing the splinter then. Oh, it's steel - no problem, you'll still be able to see it.

SHIRT COLLAR STAINS

Having problems with collar stains? Before washing the shirt, rub the collar stain vigorously with orange, grapefruit or lemon peel that you grated into a pulp.

SINK STOPPER

Lose the stopper for your sink? Substitute a plastic pill bottle of the right size, until you can find or get a new stopper.   In kitchen sinks use a small soft butter tub.   Fill it with water, set it in the drain and, while holding it in place, fill the sink with water. The water pressure will keep it there, provided you trimmed it so it doesn't stick up above the drain.

LOOSE SCREWS

Loose screw that won't tighten up? Just stick a couple of toothpicks and some glue into the hole, and drive the screw in tight...permanently.

LABEL RESIDUE

If you can't get the residue from those pesky labels off the glass, plastic, vinyl, metal or enamel items you purchased, just dab it with a cloth dipped in salad oil. In a few minutes it will come right off.

PLASTIC PIPE CUTTER

Need to cut a piece of PVC pipe and can't find your saw? If you have a piece of nylon string - use it. Lay the pipe on the floor, and using both hands, pull the string in a seesaw motion. It produces enough friction to cut through 1 inch pipe in less than a minute.

GRATING CHEESE

Before grating sticky things like cheese, rub a little salad oil on the grater. After you're done, swipe with a small brush and you can easily wash the grater clean.

STAINING WITH PAINT

If you want to paint a cement floor, buy oil based paint. Take half of the paint and mix it, one part of the paint to three parts thinner. Paint the floor with this mixture first, allow to dry, then mix the balance of your paint 50/50 with thinner and apply a second coat. By doing this, you will have stained the cement, instead of coating it. This way the paint will not peel off, and when worn, a new 50/50 coat will look great.

CLOTHES MOTHS

Worried about moths eating your stored clothing? Put 2 cups of cedar chips in a nylon stocking and pack it with your clothes. Or, hang it in the closet where you are storing clothing.

Clothes moths don't bother most of the new fabrics being made today. About the only items you need to worry about are those made of cotton or wool. If you only have a few of these things to store, try storing them in a 50 caliber ammo box. These can be purchased from most Army Surplus stores. Nice thing is they seal air tight so nothing can get inside.

POSTAGE STAMPS

Need to remove a good stamp from an envelope so you can still use it? Just cut off the corner of the envelope, leaving some paper around the stamp. Set this in a saucer of cold water and wait approximately two hours. The stamp will now slip away from the paper, easily. Set the stamp face down on a napkin or paper towel to dry. When dry, just glue it to the new envelope.
I got this tip from Frank Natale, the Postmaster at the West Middlesex Post Office.

Maybe you put the wrong check in the envelope and sealed it. Want to re-open it without losing the envelope or stamp? Just set it in the freezer for a couple of hours, take it out and slide a sharp knife under the flap and it will zip open easily. Unfortunately, you will need some glue to re-seal it.

BACILLUS THURINGIENSIS

This is a well known bacterial pest control sold under brand names like Dipel, Thuricide, etc. It's very effective controlling a number of pests, such as loopers (larvae of moths). If these little green caterpillars are a problem in your cole crop garden, buy some BT and use it to spray your plants.

Now take the infected caterpillars, about a quarter cup, and smash them in a clean small jar. Then pour in a pint of warm milk and blend them together. Allow the mixture to set for 3 days before straining through some nylon, or cheese cloth. Dilute your mixture with enough water to make a gallon of spray. Each time you spray your cole crops, collect the dead and dying caterpillars and repeat the process. Now you won't need to spend a lot of money buying Thuricide or Dipel anymore.

GARDENING TIPS

You can make a good, cheap nitrogen rich plant food by dissolving an envelope of un-flavored gelatin in a cup of hot water, then add 3 cups of cold water. Water your plants once a month with this, and they will be green and healthy.

Want to make your houseplants look great? Water them occasionally with water that you have added two teaspoons of ammonia to - they'll love it.
(2tsp. to a quart)

I've been told that soaking your tomato seed in room temperature distilled water for about 6 hours, then air drying them before planting, will increase your yield substantially. I would think this should work with other seed too.

When planting tiny seeds like carrots, dill, lettuce, etc, just spread the seeds on a cookie sheet, take a damp 12 inch piece of yarn and lay it on the seeds. The seeds stick to the string and you need only lay them end to end in the furrow, to produce a nice straight row of whatever, without wasting seeds.

Having problems with cutworms? An easy way to relieve that problem is to rototill your garden plot 3 or 4 times during the winter.

Cutworms can't tolerate freezing temperatures, so each time you till the garden you kill many of them. Rototilling over several winters, you should eliminate the problem entirely.

University studies show that tomato blossom-end rot develops due to persistently high humidity. The moist condition reduces calcium transport to the fruit. However, high humidity, only at night, favors calcium transport and reduces the rot.

PET TIPS

Pennyroyal repels fleas, or if they hang around, it kills them. Doesn't matter if it's fresh or dried, both work equally well. Put some in or under your pet's bed.

Make a flea collar by sewing a tube of some open weave material and filling it with dried pennyroyal, sew it shut and then fastening it around the pet's neck. Grow some in your yard and you will see less fleas there also.

Stray cats causing you problems? Maybe they're using your flower garden for a litter box. Cocoa Shell Mulch spread on the soil will repel most cats. Lots of cats can't stand the odor of citrus. Sometimes grinding up orange, lemon or grapefruit peels and spreading them in the garden helps - good for the soil too. Lemon Grass oil works well at repelling cats, if you can find some.

Dog chasing cars? Attach some chain to his collar that hangs down to his knees, and at the bottom attach a 4" bolt. Now every time he runs after a car the bolt will knock against his legs, causing him to stop immediately. The bolt hurts when it hits his knees while running, but as long as he walks, it's no problem.

You can stop strong doggy odor by rinsing your dog with a solution of 2 tablespoons of citronella, a ½ cup of rubbing alcohol and a gallon of water. Be sure to dry him throughly.

Giving your dog a package of yeast, or a couple of cloves of garlic, each week, spread out over several days, will keep him flea free.

If your new puppy has an accident on the rug, wash the rug with club soda. This removes the odor and the stain at the same time.

If the new puppy wants to chew the wooden furniture, just put some oil of clove where he is chewing. Think this won't work? Put a drop on your tongue.

For a quick bath on a smelly dog, rub him good with baking soda. Hold him for a minute, then put him outside to shake it off.

If your dog has a dog house, use pine needles, chamomile leaves, black walnut leaves or cedar chips for bedding, and you won't have any flea problems. Be sure to change the bedding occasionally. It loses it's effectiveness over time - with use.

Fleas cannot tolerate mint, sassafras, pennyroyal or chamomile. Boil any of these in enough water to make a strong tea and then rinse your dog with it. Just remember, a reasonable amount of fleas are good for a dog - keeps him from brooding over being a dog.

SPIDERS

Spiders comprise the largest family of arachnids. And although there are approximately 3000 species of spiders in North America, only three are harmful to humans - the black widow, the brown recluse and the yellow sac spider.

The black widow's venom is, drop for drop, the most toxic to humans.

They normally like to live in dark places, like under leaf litter, in dumps, old sheds and basements.   Any place where there is little or no traffic, or disturbances. They like it to be quiet and without any outside activity.

They are easy to recognize because of the large shiny black abdomen with the red hourglass.   You don't want to pick one up to look at it's belly, or the hour glass.   But, if it's on it's web, you may be able to see it's abdomen and the hour glass.

The brown recluse likes to be alone also, that's why he is called "recluse". People usually encounter this fellow in closets, basements, barns, attics, under furniture, in stored clothing and sometimes in things you haven't worn for several weeks.

Rarely does anybody die from this spiders bite. However, the wound may develop a necrosis, producing a large deep area of dead cell tissue. These wounds often take months to heal, leaving permanent scar tissue.

The yellow sac spider, introduced from Europe, lives almost entirely indoors and has become very common in some areas of the country. Their bite is normally not fatal, but the wound may take quite some time to heal.

Other than those spiders mentioned above, the rest are just a nuisance. Fortunately, there are some ways to control spiders in our homes. Insects and arachnids are the only creatures that I kill, and advocate that others also kill, if they're pests. The only time I kill any other creatures is to eat them, or because they have become a pest.

If you have an unfinished basement and are troubled with spiders, try this: put 2 cups of Tide laundry detergent, either liquid or powder, in a plastic bucket. Then pour a gallon of boiling water into the bucket and stir until all the detergent is suspended in the water.

When the solution is cool, spray all the corners in your basement. Remember, every L is an inside corner - where floor meets walls, walls meet ceiling, wall meets wall, around door and window frames, etc. If you do a good job, you won't see a spider in the basement for up to 10 weeks.

Every fall as soon as the night time temperature drops below freezing, you can collect some Osage Oranges. These will keep spiders out of your home until next spring.

Locate an Osage Orange tree, and don't tell anybody if you want to get some of the oranges. Now watch the weather reports on T V, and when they predict a freeze is coming that night, go and remove all the oranges from under the tree.

Tomorrow, every orange you find on the ground will have been knocked from the tree by the frost. And that is what is needed to make them work. In a 9X12 room, you will need 4 baseball sized oranges or 2 softball sized oranges.

As the oranges decay, they give off an essence that repels insects and arachnids, so don't throw them out unless they start to grow a mold, that looks like cotton over 25% of the orange. This mold can be white, yellow or gray and, if allowed to continue growing, will attract fruit flies.

SKUNKS

Sometimes you need to catch a skunk, or you catch one by accident trying to catch some other animal.

Nevertheless, there is a skunk in your cage trap and you need to get it out without it spraying e v e r y t h i n g, i n c l u d i n g you...right?

This is what you will need. One large blanket you can't see through, one large plastic leaf bag, a yellow pencil and a can of "Starting Fluid". With your arms out stretched, hold the blanket up in front of you so nothing shows but your eyes and your feet.

Start toward the trap slowly, and if it starts to raise it's tail, stop and stand still until it lowers it's tail again. Continue forward again, until you are standing at the trap. Slowly lower the blanket and cover the trap completely.

You can now pick up the trap and take it to a table or the tailgate of your truck. Set the trap down, being careful to keep the blanket from getting caught under the trap.

Next, open the leaf bag and arrange it in front of the trap so that you can stand at the back of the trap and pull the blanket off of the trap while you pull the leaf bag on to the trap. (Setting a short 2X4 under the trap helps.) If you carefully pull on the blanket and the bag at the same time, you can be removing one while installing the other. Once you have the trap in the bag, you are ready to put the skunk to sleep, permanently.

Many states require you to kill these animals because of the chance of spreading rabies when you release the animal someplace else. If your state allows you to transport and release these animals, don't bother putting the trap in the bag. Just take it to where you intend to release the animal. Set the trap on the ground and stand at the end opposite the door. Slowly pull the blanket back until the door end is uncovered.

Gently raise the door without letting the skunk see you, and prop it open by sliding a rod from one side to the other.

Now go back to the truck and sit down It may take 10 or 15 minutes before the skunk gets enough nerve to leave the trap. After it's gone, get your trap, and you're done.

If you must destroy the skunk, take the pencil and poke a hole in the bag. Put one squirt of the "Starting Fluid" in the hole and seal the hole with the masking tape. Wait 10 minutes, poke another hole and give it 2 squirts and seal it. Wait for 15 minutes, then lift one end of the trap to tell if the skunk is still awake. If he is awake, you can feel him moving around inside the trap. If he's sleeping, you may feel him slide along the bottom, if you hold it high enough.

If it is awake, repeat the last squirts. If it's asleep, poke another hole, fill the bag with fluid and seal the hole. In about 30 minutes it will be dead and you can bury the animal. To keep another animal from digging up the skunk, put it in the hole you have dug, and pour kerosene over it before you fill in the hole. The smell of the kerosene keeps other animals from investigating, by masking the odor of decaying flesh. Even though you can't smell it, animals can when they sniff the freshly dug dirt. If you don't have kerosene, put some large rocks on top of the skunk before you fill in the hole with dirt.

HOUSEHOLD TIPS

Spray your plastic food containers with a non-stick cooking spray before using to store tomato based foods. I've been told that holding the container under real cold water before filling works also. At least that is what a listener from Mercer said. Right, Dorothy?

When a recipe calls for flouring the baking pan, use some of the cake mix instead, and there won't be any white residue on the cake.

To keep celery longer, wrap it in aluminum foil when putting it in the refrigerator.

To bring out the natural sweetness of corn, put a small amount of sugar in the water you boil it in.

My wife stores her spare electric extension cords in paper towel tubes she saves when the towels are all used..

Your S. O. S. pads will last longer if you buy the junior size and then cut them in half. You will also notice that your scissors will be sharper too.

To remove burnt food from your skillet, just add a little dish soap and enough water to cover the bottom. Bring to a boil, then cool a little and wipe clean.

Need to clean the toilet, but no bowl cleaner? No problem, just drop in a couple of Alka-Seltzer tablets. Wait 5 minutes, brush and flush.

If you put your false teeth in effervescent denture cleanser to clean them, just dump the water into the toilet bowl and you won't need to clean the bowl so often.

Spray some perfume on the light bulb in a lamp and the room will have a nice "light" scent.

Loose chair rungs can be tightened, just like new, with a few drops of old fashion anti-freeze applied to the rung. Make sure the rung isn't completely covered with glue. Replace it in it's pocket and clamp over night. In the morning it will be as good as new.

Dryer fabric softener sheets repel moths and impart a freshly washed smell to the clothes in your dresser drawers or closet. If you attached one to your hat, shirt sleeves, cuffs or the back of your shirt collar, biting insects will not come near you.

To stop the itch from mosquito bites, rub some soap on them and allow it to dry.... Immediately, No Itch!

CHIPMUNKS

There are a lot of people that think chipmunks are cute and harmless, that is until they start knocking down

stone walls or tipping over the condenser of the air conditioner, by digging under these things. Then they want them gone.

I've used the following method for more years than I care to think about and haven't found anything that works better.

Get a 10 foot section of thin wall sewer pipe, 4" in diameter, and cut it into 5 equal sections, 24" long. These are to be used as bait stations. Now mix 2 tablespoons of RO-DEX in a cup of peanut butter, to be used for bait. These items will mix easier if you microwave the peanut butter for about 20 seconds.

When throughly mixed, place the bait in the freezer to harden, approximately 20 minutes. When the bait is stiff enough to work with, using a spoon, place a chunk the size of a walnut in the center of each of the bait stations you're using.

You have probably seen chipmunks dashing from one place to another. Did you ever wonder why they never walk anyplace? It's because they are afraid of everything, and can't be caught out in the open. Just about every other small animal, and some birds, will kill, and sometimes eat him, if they get the chance.

Knowing these things should alert you to the fact that where you put the bait stations is most important. You must place the bait station where the chipmunks will not be afraid to go into them, like under shrubs, up against the house or garage, any place that is protected. Put yourself in their shoes when placing the stations. If I were his size, and everything wanted to eat me, would I linger here? If the answer is yes, put down a station. If the answer is no, better find a better location or you won't find the bait eaten. If they don't eat the bait, you will never solve your problem.

Remember, the Good Lord never lets you win the war, just some of the battles. That, my friend, means don't throw your stations away when fall comes. Next summer, and the next summer and every summer thereafter, you will need them. Especially if your neighbors don't use the method on their property.

SEWER & FRUIT FLIES

Sewer flies and fruit flies are both members of the gnat family and look alike to the naked eye. If you want to be able to tell the difference, get a good 10 power magnifying glass. The fruit fly is tobacco brown with two large, clay red eyes. The sewer fly, on the other hand, is black and is covered with white hairs.

Sewer flies love to lay their eggs in your drains. When the eggs hatch, the larvae feed on the scum inside of the drain pipes until they enter the pupae stage. When they hatch as adult flies, they leave the drain to breed. Then they return to the drain to lay their eggs and that is how you get infested. These flies don't live more than several days, but lay enough eggs to infest you in a very short time.

Fruit flies usually hang around fruit or garbage, and aren't interested in your drains. That is why you should cover your garbage, and why I always advise people to dip fruit into a bath of water containing some chlorine bleach. This kills the eggs and larvae, if there are any on the fruit.

Sewer flies are always found around the sink drain. Now that you know the difference, you can decide which you have, and if they are sewer flies, do the following:

In the evening just before you go to bed, pour 1 cup of chlorine bleach down every drain in the house, except floor drains, use 2 for these drains. Then cover each drain with an old rag that is soaking wet. Fold the rag into a pad, but do not wring it out, it must be soaked to make a good seal. In the morning check each rag, if it's been bleached white your problem is solved.

If it's not bleached, then you need to find out why, correct the problem, and try again. Sometimes the rag wasn't wet enough or you didn't lay it flat enough to seal the drain. Or maybe the drain has a leak at water level and the gas got out, but you don't notice any water leaking or see any evidence of a leak.

BATS

I have never understood why so many people are afraid of bats. Check the next fifty people you meet and I'll bet you don't find one that can tell you a true story of a bat hurting them.   On the other hand, ask them if they have ever been bitten by a dog and I bet you that you hear lots of dog stories.

Bats are very beneficial to people and should not be indiscriminately killed. Every time a bat goes out for it's evening flight, it eats thousands of insects. In fact, the little brown bat eats between 2000 and 3000 insects every night it's out flying. Do the numbers on that, if you had 50 bats - get an idea of the benefits we reap from having bats in our neighborhood?

Bats being mammals, cannot survive winter in the colder northern parts of the country, therefore they either hibernate or fly south for the winter. In fact, bats are one of the very few creatures that are true hibernators.

In the fall, as winter weather approaches, they either fly south or go to the same place to hibernate that they use every year. During hibernation, they drop into a deep death like sleep. Their heart beats, and they breath only 2 or 3 times a minute. Their body temperature drops to approximately 50° and they appear to be dead.

In this state, having dropped their metabolism, they survive by living off the fat they have stored up in their bodies. However, should something wake them before spring, when insects are available, their metabolism goes up and they consume too much of the fat stored in their bodies. Because of this, many could die of starvation before spring and the insects arrive.

Forget the old wives tales about the filthy, lice ridden, loathsome bats. Bats are very clean animals, grooming themselves constantly. They don't carry lice nor do they tangle themselves in ladies hair.

New homes, being so well insulated and tightly built, have few problems with bats. It's the older homes that seem to have most of the problems. If you are one of those people that need help with a bat problem, let me give you some solutions.

The first thing you need to do is locate the entrances that the bats are using to get into your house. Starting just before dusk, station yourself at one corner of the house and your spouse at the opposing corner. This way you each can see two different walls of the house.

Make sure you and the spouse have a pencil and a tablet with a drawing of each of the walls you are watching. When either of you see bats exiting the house, mark the approximate location on the drawing. That way, you can locate the openings in the daylight.

You must stay at your station until total darkness, to be sure you have seen all of the openings being used. Now that you know where the bats are getting in, we can do something to stop them.

Get a 24" high roll of hardware cloth with ¼" holes, a staple gun, staples, a roll of duct tape and some black plastic bags. Using a ladder, get up and check out the openings. If bats are using them, they will be smooth, like they were sand papered, and darker than the surrounding area.

Okay, this is the place. Measure the opening and look at it throughly, considering how you will be able to install the no-return you will build to fit.

Let's say the opening is eight inches wide, between the fascia and soffit boards. That means the no-return needs to be a tunnel. Put the hardware cloth aside and get a black plastic bag. Cut the bottom out so that you have a tube, and slit the sides down about 3". With the duct tape, tape one side of the slit end to the fascia board and the other end to the soffit board.

Using the duct tape, make sure there are no holes for light to shine inside the tube. With the tunnel hanging down loose, the bats can drop out, but can't find a way to get back in. They will normally hang around for several days and then leave. Don't be too quick to take the tunnel down, they could check back later - maybe they don't like their new home.

Now, let's say that the hole is at the edge of the roof, where the roof meets the fascia board. You can still use the bag method. Let's say another opening is along the side of the house, where the soffit meets the wall. Cut a piece of hardware cloth 18" inches long and fold it into a tunnel shape.

Fold the hardware cloth so that you have a tunnel 10" wide and 2" deep and 24" long. Let me walk you through this. Along the 24" side of the wire, fold a 2" wide strip. Next fold another 2" strip, in the opposite direction. On the other side of the 24" strip, do the same thing. You should now have a tunnel to set against the wall - tight up against the soffit. Staple it in place and make sure there isn't any way in or out, except through the bottom opening.

If necessary, use the duct tape to be sure there are not openings around the top of the tunnel. The bats move down the wire, drop out and fly away. However, upon returning, they can't find the way back in. Don't remove the tunnel for a year or so, they may just stop by to see about moving back in.

Sorry, but if you have a slate or tile roof, these methods will not help you. The bats slip into your attic by going under the slate or the tile. Your only hope is to seal the roof, or replace it.

If you have decided to seal it, fine, try this. Cut strips of ¼" plywood wide enough to just fit between the roof rafters. Allowing for the plywood, on one rafter, nail a ¾" scab of wood to hold the plywood in place. Now slip the plywood into place, set another scab on the other rafter and nail it in place. Do the entire roof this way.

LADY BUGS

Otherwise known as lady bird beetles, or Asian Beetles, seem to be a problem for lots of people now days. You probably already know that these insects are not native to our country. They were imported from somewhere in Asia, and as you probably already know, winter-over in the walls of houses and other buildings.

The reason, I believe, that these insects winter over in buildings is because in Asia they don't have trees with bark or leaves, like ours. Their trees have tight, smooth bark, no place to hide there. And those trees don't produce leaf litter the way ours do.

Actually, you probably don't care about that; you just want to know how to keep them out of your house. The best thing you can do is try to keep them from your living quarters. I can help you with that, if you follow my instructions. First, remember what my daddy said; "nothing works until you do."

Using a clear caulk, lay a bead along the top and bottom of every baseboard. Next do the same thing around every door frame and every window. By caulking these things, you close up the way they are getting into your living quarters. You might want to take the covers off the outlets and light switches and seal the openings of these also, if the plate doesn't lay flat on the wall. They will still get under the siding and into the attic, but not into the living quarters.

Usually, before these insects go under the siding, they gather on the outside of the siding for a day or so. This allows you the opportunity to kill lots of them, thereby, relieving the problem, somewhat, for next year. You see, these insects don't lay their eggs until they come out of dormancy in the spring. So killing some now, kills many for the future. I understand that this is a rather large job, but you know what my Daddy always said, "nothing works until you do!"

So here is what you do. Go buy yourself a Hot Pepper Wax Brand hose end sprayer. Attach it to your garden hose and fill the jar with Tide laundry detergent. Set the nozzle to the small round hole, the stream setting. Then set the mixture knob, located on the top, for a 32 to 1 mixture. Starting at one corner of the house, begin spraying the wall from the top to the bottom. As you move around the house, make certain that you have sprayed the corner posts, window frames and door frames, throughly. If you have done the job properly, you will have killed lots of these pests.

One last thought. If you can put up with these critters, they will eat plenty of the bad bugs that are eating our plants. In fact, some say that these insects will eventually be regulated by the amount of food available to them. I guess that means that when they have eaten most of the bad bugs, then their numbers will drop significantly. If that is true, then sooner or later these critters will eat themselves out of existence. "Maybe you would be interested in buying a bridge I have for sale?"

GROUND HOGS

Ground hogs can be a pain in the butt when they decide to move in on your garden. I don't mind sharing, but when they take the best of everything, I call that war. To eliminate these pests, you will need a 5' section of stiff hose, a cotton sock, a funnel, a quart of ammonia and a quart of chlorine bleach. Locate their main entrance hole. Somewhere within a 12' radius of that hole, you will usually find one or more other holes, in the high grass, with no dirt out front. These are escape holes, fill them in with some of the dirt from the main entrance, and tamp the soil good.

Stick the sock on the end of the hose and carefully shove the hose, with the sock on the end, down the main entrance hole. Push it in as far as you can, but don't pull it back, you could lose the sock and ruin the whole system. When the hose is in as far as it will go, fill in the entrance hole with the dirt surrounding it, being careful not to pull on the hose. Tamp the dirt down solid and stick the funnel in the end of the hose. Now pour all of the bleach and then the ammonia down the hose. Pull the hose out and tamp the little hole shut with your foot. This is one ground hog that will never see daylight again. NEVER PUT CHLORINE BLEACH AND AMMONIA TOGETHER IN ANYTHING ABOVE GROUND!

Combined together these two items make chlorine gas-a deadly poison if you breath it. Using my method will not harm you, because the chlorine bleach and ammonia don't get mixed until they meet under ground. Chlorine gas is heavier than air so can't come up out of the ground. Follow the instructions, to the letter, and you will not have any problems.

RATS

Seems like more and more folks are having problems with rats getting into their homes, especially around businesses like grocery stores, fast food places and restaurants. Sometimes people try poisoning these pest with disastrous results. Very few commercial poisons will kill rats quickly enough to keep them from getting back into the walls of your house before they die.

When a rat dies inside of a wall, you are in for some real bad odor problems. I always advise anybody with rodent problems, of any kind, not to use poison inside their homes. If you want to use poison, make sure the rats can't carry it back into your walls, eat it and die.

Many times you will find that the rats have become acclimated to the poison and it no longer kills them. Another problem with most poisons is that the rats carry it away and hide it someplace, instead of eating it. Maybe that's why they call them "pack rats."

I know of one farmer that used a five gallon bucket full of rat poison, and found out some months later when expanding his barn, that they hadn't eaten hardly any of it. He gathered up enough to almost refill the bucket.

Let me give you my method for dealing with rats. When we lived in Pittsburgh, some time back, we were invaded by rats when they closed and tore down West View Amusement Park. After some extensive investigation, I discovered that rodents can't belch, throw up or pass gas. I also learned that they haven't any saliva glands, making their mouth as dry as your palm. After quite a bit of thought, I decide to use this information against them. All I needed to do was "gas them up," and...Bang! Just how do I do that? Easy. Feed them instant dried potatoes sprinkled with powdered Alka Seltzer tablets. Place a little water close by so that they can relieve their thirst and.....Bam! Dead rat! And guess what, they never become acclimated to this stuff, like they do with commercial poisons. And they don't get far after drinking some water, so you usually find them close to the water - dead!

TRAPPER TALES

The lady I live with now, my second wife, otherwise known as "my keeper," said that if I were to write a book entitled "The Best of Trapper John," it must contain some of my stories. Since I agreed to put some stories in this book, I thought you should know that all of them are true. I hope most of my readers enjoy reading them, as much as I have enjoyed telling them.

P.S. "I know these are true because I have heard them 'soo' many times - they don't change."

John's "KEEPER"

CLYDE THE RACCOON

Way back when I still lived in Pittsburgh, I was an avid hunter and trapper; same as now. One day I saw an ad in the Pittsburgh Press; some guy was offering to give 4 raccoons to whoever purchased the large cage that they were living in. Boy, I just couldn't resist an offer like that, so I bought the cage. There were 3 females and one male.

Several months after I made the purchase and transported the whole shebang back home, one of the females gave birth to 3 pups. Well, I always wanted to have a pet raccoon, so I brought the male into the house to raise. Of course, my wife fed it, and it naturally formed an attachment to her. I guess he thought she was his mother.

We decided to call him "Clydie," and as he grew, he would run and climb up my wife's leg anytime something scared him. Time went by and Cldyie got heavier, and this became a problem. Especially, when the wife was wearing sweatpants. Well, the day finally arrived when something scared him while we had company. Up her leg he went, down came her pants......Oh Boy, Naked Wife!

It wasn't long before Clydie learned how to open the cabinets under the kitchen sink. He thought this was great, his own hiding place. Then he found a way to get up into the silverware drawer.

We had a good time with that little trick every time we had company. We would go into the kitchen and make sure that our guest sat next to the counter by the silverware drawer. The wife would pour coffee for everybody and I would ask our guest to get us some teaspoons from the silverware drawer. The guest would pull the drawer open and Clydie would raise hell and pull it closed. You should've seen the expression on their faces.....Funny!

One Saturday, my wife had two gentlemen come by the house to take pictures of the kids. (Some kind of offer from one of the local studios.) While one of them was talking to the wife, the other sat on the sofa. All of a sudden the man on the sofa got this funny look on his face - like he was sick. I asked, "are you okay?" Stuttering, he said, "something is holding my leg." "Oh, that's alright, it's just Clyde." I never saw anybody move so fast in my entire life! They were gone in the blink of an eye. Never could get them to come back and take any pictures.

Clydie, being a raccoon, loved to play in water and never missed a chance. One evening while my wife was cooking supper, she decided to wash some dishes. And as usual, Clydie climbed up on the counter between the stove and sink. Now get this picture: the gas stove is to the left, there is a 12" wide counter and then the double bowl sink. Clydie always sat there, because the drawer pulls made it easy to climb up that counter.

So, there sat Clydie playing in the water and chittering to my wife. Suddenly Clydie started sniffing the air and getting excited. Looking back, he saw that his tail was on fire, made a strange noise, grabbed his tail with one hand, and with the other beat the flames, momentarily. Then, as he plunged his tail into the water in the sink, he proceeded to bite my wife's arm, for not watching his tail more closely.

Remember, your mother is responsible for everything that happens to you - at least that is what Clydie believed.

Unfortunately, we couldn't go out and leave Clydie loose at home. If you forgot, he would help you to remember next time, by taking down the curtains, drapes, or maybe removing everything from the kitchen cabinets. We took to putting Clydie in the laundry room, when we had to leave the house for any length of time.

One day after finishing a small job in the basement, we had one 1 X 4 X 8 sheet of white Styrofoam board left. Steven said, " Dad, what do you want to do with this Styrofoam?" "Stick it behind the furnace," I told him, and forgot about it. A week or so later, we had to leave Clydie in the laundry room, where the furnace also resided. When we arrived home, I went to let Clydie out, but, upon opening the door, I was confronted with tons of small white balls the size of BB's. The room was full to overflowing.

I had no idea that one single Styrofoam board could, when dismantled, fill an 8 X 8 X 8 room, from floor to ceiling. When we finally got all of those little balls stuffed into plastic bags, we discovered Clydie sitting on the one wall between the rafters waiting for us to return.

Another time, my wife forgot she had left a 10 lb bag of potatoes under the laundry tubs. We left Clydie in the laundry room for the evening and upon returning, were happy to find him sitting there and everything else in order - NO TROUBLE! In the morning, the wife went to the laundry room to do some wash and found the room flooded. Standing in 2" of water, I removed the lid over the sewer drain and tried to run a snake down the drain.

The snake wouldn't go in more than several inches before hitting something. Using a piece of   re-bar, I dug out a potato! You should have seen the look on my face when they all popped up out of the drain. "Where the hell did he get these potatoes," I said, to nobody in particular. "Oh, my god," exclaimed my wife, "I forgot, I put them under the laundry tubs the other day." To make a long story short, Clydie somehow stuffed 10 lbs of potatoes down the floor drain and replaced the lid.

Then there was the time I made the clay Frankenstein head for Steven's Halloween costume. About 6:30 on Halloween evening, the doorbell rang. Since Steven was dressed and ready, with Clydie around his neck, he answered the door. As he opened the door, two adult men with two small children jumped back, startled.

One of the adults laughed, saying, "Great costume!"
Just then Clydie lifted his head and growled. Steven
yelled, "Hey, you guys didn't get any candy," as they
disappeared down the road. Guess they decided to try
getting their candy someplace else.

Unfortunately, Clydie decided that my shoes were the
perfect toilet. Talk about Surprise! Surprise! We
tried to break this habit, but couldn't get anywhere
with Clydie - he just wouldn't stop. That, as they say,
was the straw that broke the camel's back. " Clydie,
you are out of here!" "Put an ad in the paper, free to a
good home and give him to the first person that
answers the ad!"

A week or so later, I returned from work to have my
wife greet me with, " A fellow came and took Clydie
this afternoon." "Good," I said, feeling a little
remorse, knowing that I wouldn't see him anymore.
That evening I was watching the 11:00 news when
there was a knock on the front door. I opened the door
and there stood a young man, covered with scratches.
"What happened, can I help you?" I asked, "was there
an accident?"

"No, I just brought him back," he answered me.
"Who?" I asked. "Him!" he said, as he pointed at the
ground behind him. There sat Clydie in his travel cage.
I reached down and opened the door. Clydie shot by
me and flew up the steps, down the hall and into the
closet.

169

The fellow said, " Sorry, my mother said that I can't keep him, all he wants to do is eat me." I guess I can keep my shoes in the foot locker a little longer.

Eventually, we gave Clydie to a fellow that had a petting Zoo for kids. He seemed to like having all of those kid fuss over him. And I certainly loved being able to leave my shoes under the bed, without being surprised.

LIFE WITH A PIG

We moved to the farm in Mercer in December of 1978, and I went to work for McRea Electric in Grove City doing refrigeration and appliance repairs. In February of 1980, I went to a lady's house near Slippery Rock to repair a refrigerator. As I was heading for the refrigerator, I noticed a very small piglet in a cardboard box by the electric range. "Trying to raise a pig for yourself?"I asked. "No,"she answered. "Jim is stopping over to put it down; there's something wrong with it." "Seems like a shame," I said. "You can take it with you if you like, maybe you can raise it." When I finished, I picked up the box and left. That evening, after trying for quite some time to get the little fellow to eat, we decided it was useless, he would die.

I walked across the road to invite the two little boys that lived there to come over and see the piglet before it died. Their father, John, a chiropractor, came over with the kids a short time later. The father looked into the box, turned to me and said, "It needs adjusted." "You're the chiropractor," I said. "Go ahead and adjust him." "Get me a bath towel," he said, as he picked the piglet up. I handed him a towel and he laid the piglet on it, on the kitchen table. Next thing I could hear was what sounded like somebody cracking their knuckles. The piglet jumped to it's feet and started squealing for something to eat. "He'll need adjusted a couple more times, I'll stop tomorrow," said John.

That was the beginning of life with "Ozzie Pig." As Ozzie grew, we noticed that her (yes, he was a her) left hind leg was shorter than the rest of her legs. As she got heavier we found that she was not able to come up the steps into the house any longer. She kept losing her balance and falling over.

At this time she weighed around 70 pounds, so we decided it was just as well that she get used to living outside. I built her an A-frame 6' wide and 8' long, hoping it would fit for a lifetime. Unfortunately, Ozzie wasn't too keen on living outside, and since the steps were no good to her, she just removed them - turning them into kindling in the process. Well, we needed new steps anyway, right?

As Ozzie got used to living outside, she started following my wife around the place. This seemed to work out pretty good; as the wife weeded the vegetable garden, Ozzie ate the weeds.

One day Ozzie mistakenly ate the tops of something and the wife slapped her. Ozzie was MAD! She spun around in circles until she fell over, jumped up and ran for her house. A little while later my wife looked behind her and there was Ozzie eating the vegetables - not the weeds. The wife yelled and swatted Ozzie, who paid no attention, just kept on eating. My wife run to the house, got a broom and run back to the garden. She started smacking Ozzie with the broom. Ozzie went into her spinning routine, fell over, jumped up, ran down the row of vegetables and threw herself on one of my wife's cabbages, squashing it flat. She nonchalantly got up and walked back to her house and laid down. This became Ozzie's way of "getting even" with my wife when she did anything Ozzie felt she shouldn't.

One afternoon, the girls were going shopping, and I elected to stay home to hold down the fort, as they say. At that time we had several cats, two large dogs, one young turkey and Ozzie running around the place. I was sitting on the front porch reading, when hunger arrived. I went in and got a loaf of fresh baked whole wheat bread and returned to the porch.

Sitting back down, I noticed I was being stared at, by the animals. I guessed they were hungry too, so I sat on the steps and shared my bread with them. As we sat there eating, the turkey decided that it should sit on my head, where it might get more food. Paying little attention, I kept reading, eating and feeding them.

The feeling that I was being watched came over me and I looked up. There in a car, on the road in front of the house sat a man and lady staring at us. There I sat with a young turkey perched on my head, a cat in my lap, a very large dog on both sides and a big pig sitting in front of me. I smiled. The car lunged forward down the road approximately 50 yards, stopped dead in it's tracks, the man stuck his head out the window, looked back, and I waved as he raced away down the road.

Funny thing about pigs; they take on the behavior of the animals they pal around with, such as dogs. We had a 185 pound rottweiler, Buck, and Max, who was half rottweiler and half wolf and almost as big. Both dogs believed the place belonged to them and were not afraid to tell you about it when you came on the property. There was a lady that loved to ride her horse and would sometimes cross our fields. Of course, when she did, the dogs went out to give her the devil for being in their field. One day, we noticed that Ozzie was following the dogs wolfing at the top of her lungs. At first we laughed about the stupid pig thinking it was a dog.

There was a fellow that worked for me for awhile, and Buck didn't like him, for some reason that I didn't understand. Every time Buck saw this fellow, he would show his teeth. He never did anything, just show teeth.

Then, one day while Buck was showing his teeth, Ozzie decided to go after the fellow in earnest. I arrived just in time to halt any problems before they happened. The final episode came when Ozzie cornered the UPS driver in his truck. A 585 pound pig can do lots of damage if it decided it didn't like you. After that we penned her up and she turned mean to everybody. We had to have her destroyed. It broke my heart to have to do that to something that loved me, and I loved. But, I learned a hard lesson that I won't forget.

SNAKE IN THE TUB

One evening some years ago, colder than *#%* outside, I was sitting in my cozy living room watching television, when the telephone rang. Picking up the receiver, I heard a trembling female voice saying, "Is this Trapper John?" "Yes mam, I'm Trapper John. What can I do for you?" "There's a big snake in my bathtub," she says! "Yea, who is this?" I asked. "I'm serious, you gotta come right away!"

"Come where?" I asked. When she told me, I said, "Lady, that's a half hour drive, I would have to load my equipment; probably take me an hour to get there." "Listen," she said," I live in a trailer on....road and there is a VERY big snake in my tub. I need your help, please!" "Have your husband get rid of it," I told her. "Please, I don't have a husband, I need your help, please!" " Okay, I'll get there as soon as I can."

I loaded the proper equipment and headed for her place. As I turned onto her road, some fifty minutes later, I came face to face with a naked blue lady, standing in a yard, holding a portable telephone. I pulled into the drive, stopped and jumped out of the truck taking off my jacket. Putting my jacket around her shoulders, I suggested she sit in the truck where it was warm, while I see about the snake. Sliding the tub door open, I could see a rather large (about 5') black rat snake in the tub. I put it in my snake box and went back outside to the truck. "It's okay now, you can go inside." "Not until you check the entire trailer; I'm not getting out of this truck." Setting the box in the back of the truck, I returned to the trailer and checked every room - no more snakes. Walking back out to the truck, I noticed a shadow coming across the road. It was the lady that lived across the road and she agreed to stay with my customer for awhile. We all walked back to the trailer and they went in. I waited at the door.

They went into the bedroom, and when they returned the lady had clothes on and my money in her hand. She thanked me, paid me and I, and my jacket, went home. I turned the snake loose in my basement and he lived there until spring, when I let him go near the barn.

WHAT'S IN A NAME

Folks are constantly asking how I came to be called Trapper John. Let me tell you how it all got started, way back when I was 11 years old. One morning, while walking to school through a neighbor's farm, I was going down the lane past a shed, when I noticed somebody inside. Peaking inside, I saw that it was Al, the farmer, skinning a rat. "Why are you skinning that rat?" I asked. He smiled and said, "Come on over here and feel it." I touched the pelt and was surprised at how soft it was."Boy, the rats in our barn don't feel like that," I said. He laughed and said, "This is a muskrat, not a barn rat, and I'm skinning it to sell the pelt." "For how much?" I asked. "I get 85 cents for one this size," he answered. "Where do you get them?" I asked. "I trap them," he said, "Are you interested in learning how?" "You bet I am (85 cents was a fortune to a kid back then)," I shouted. "You be at my back door tomorrow morning at 6:00 AM and you can have these two traps and I'll show you where and how to set them."

At 6:00 AM the next morning, I was standing on his back step waiting. He took me down to the spring run on his property and showed me some of the holes that the muskrats lived in. We set my two traps in the spring run - one at an entrance hole and the other one at a feed station, using a piece of apple for bait. On the way home from school, I checked the traps and, "Holly Molly," there was a dead muskrat in one of them. Snatching it up I ran to find Al. After he finished skinning it and placing it on a stretcher board, he handed me 55 cents. "I thought you said they were worth 85 cents," I said. "That's for one that's skinned and dried, but since I have to skin and dry them for you, you get 55 cent - okay?" That, as they say, was the beginning of a life-long passion for trapping.

When I was growing up, everybody had a nickname. Since I trapped, my friends called me "Trapper"- it fit! On into the seventies, when CB radio was the rage, you needed a handle - your radio name. Well, Trapper John worked for me. In time the title just seemed to stick with some of my friends. When I started doing Animal Damage Control Trapping, and my radio show, it just seemed to fit - again.

CONTACTING TRAPPER

Sometimes people want to talk directly to me about a problem, but don't want to call my radio show. While I appreciate their feelings and desire to have me personally handle their problem, they must realize that I can't be all things to everybody. I have a wife and a personal life, and no desire to set these aside. Feeling this way, leads me to the conclusion that it is impossible to take telephone calls at home and still be fair to my wife. Consequently, I never take calls at home. If you are having a problem and want to discuss it with me, you will have to call the radio show.

If you have access to the "World Wide Web", you can contact me through my website, www.asktrapperjohn.com . Answering e-mail is very time consuming when you get as many as I do, so don't expect a response for several weeks. By the way, I don't respond to foolish e-mails.

For those folks that don't have access to the World Wide Web, you can write to me at my home, and if you enclose a self-addressed, stamped envelope with your question, I'll send you a response to the question.

Trapper John
3229 Frampton Road
West Middlesex, Pa. 16159-3107

To Order Additional Books
send your check to:

Trapper John Inc.
3229 Frampton Road
West Middlesex, Pa. 16159-3107

Each book is $25.00, postage paid

Make your check payable to
Trapper John Inc.

All books are sent first class mail

To arrange for Trapper to speak to your group,
or to appear at your organization's function, call

724 528 2073

or send an e-mail to:
trapper@asktrapperjohn.com

NOTES

NOTES

NOTES